Persons and Persuasions

Persons and Persuasions

OREN ROOT

W · W · NORTON & COMPANY · INC·

NEW YORK

Copyright © 1974 by Oren Root

FIRST EDITION

Library of Congress Cataloging in Publication Data

Root, Oren, 1911–
   Persons and persuasions.

   1. Root, Oren, 1911–   2. Willkie, Wendell
Lewis, 1892–1944. 3. New York (State)—Politics and
government—1951–   4. Rockefeller, Nelson Aldrich,
1908–   I. Title.
E748.R69A36   320.9'747'04   73–12232
ISBN 0–393–07482–X

Published simultaneously in Canada
by George J. McLeod Limited, Toronto

Some of the material in the early part of Chapter Four was first published
in *The Atlantic Monthly* in slightly different form.

The author wishes to thank Anthony Root for taking the photograph which
appears on the jacket and for reproducing other illustrations in the book.

PRINTED IN THE UNITED STATES OF AMERICA

1 2 3 4 5 6 7 8 9 0

DEDICATION

To my colleagues at the law firm of
Barrett Smith Schapiro & Simon
whose friendship and generosity
contributed importantly to this book

Contents

Acknowledgments

In the writing of a book many people necessarily play a part, often an indispensable part. Among those who contributed to this book, I want to mention Betty Bell Apel; John J. Barrett; Charles D. Breitel; Anne Fremantle; Mrs. Alan Kirk; Wesley Lindow; Charles M. Metzner; Elisabeth Luce Moore; Maria Shrady; David Simon; Debbie Simon; Linda Storrow; Gus Tyler; Charles A. Williams, Jr.; my children, Oren, Spyros, Dolores, and Anthony, and Oren's wife, Barbara; and especially my wife, Daphne. The persons named either conferred with me concerning the book or reviewed part or all of the manuscript. In some cases they made suggestions of style or substance, and in all cases they gave me moral and psychic support. To them, and to those others who helped whom I have not named, I express my deepest gratitude. I also want to say thanks to my editor, Evan Thomas, and to my agent, Sterling Lord, who have held my hand with sympathetic understanding during my first book-length literary effort.

July 10, 1973

Persons and Persuasions

Wendell Willkie— The Great Crusade

I

From time to time in human history a meteor of unusual brilliance flashes across the sky. Wendell L. Willkie was such a meteor. Thirty-three years have passed since he ran for president of the United States, twenty-nine years since he died. He was defeated when he was the Republican nominee in 1940 and in 1944 he was defeated in his effort to be nominated by the Republicans a second time. A few months after his 1944 defeat, he contracted an infection of the throat, which was followed by a weakening of the heart and that was followed by death. Yet today his name and his charisma survive well beyond that of many others whose time is more recent and whose careers by some standards

15

were more successful. His story is worthy of analysis, and, since I had the good fortune to play a part in that story, I record here some of the things I know.

To understand Wendell Willkie the public person, one must recreate the political situation in early 1940 in the United States and in the world. The world was in the midst of the "phony war." In 1939 Hitler had invaded Poland. After accepting the Anschluss with Austria and after standing by during the rape of Czechoslovakia, England and France had finally declared war against Germany. But after that nothing much happened. The French dug in behind the Maginot Line, Prime Minister Chamberlain continued to bumble away in the United Kingdom, and the German legions waited for their next move. The United States, of course, was not yet in the war, and there were many in our country who did not take the war in Europe seriously.

A personal reminiscence may give something of the flavor of that time. Herbert Hoover, the former president of the United States, came one night in early 1940 to address the Young Republican Club of New York, of which I was a member, and to answer questions. Only questions in writing were acceptable to Mr. Hoover, and after his introductory talk he ran through them as one would shuffle a deck of cards. In due course he came to a question which asked what should be the policy of the United States in the event that the independence or indeed the existence of England and France were to be put in serious jeopardy by the German arms. As that question came to the top of President Hoover's deck he dismissed it with the comment that it was too impossible an event to warrant comment.

That was the winter of 1940. But in May 1940 Hitler's armies rolled across Belgium and Holland and into France. On June 14 Paris fell to the Germans and the Führer danced a jig before the Arc de Triomphe, the picture of which will never be erased from the minds of any person who then saw it. On June 28 Wendell Willkie, who had never held any public office and who four years before had voted for the Democratic candidate, was nominated by the Republican party for president. The events were not unconnected.

To understand fully what happened we must search further. Why Wendell Willkie? What were the alternatives? Was the nomination a true draft or did Willkie seek it, perhaps connive for it? Was the nomination something which came truly from the grass roots or was it engineered by power brokers of the Eastern Establishment? For many these questions have never been adequately answered and for history's sake they need answers.

We have sketched the situation in the world in the winter and spring of 1940. What was the situation in the United States? Franklin D. Roosevelt, having swept forty-six of the forty-eight states in the election of 1936, was president. Largely as a consequence of his leadership, the country had withdrawn from the edge of economic collapse and perhaps social revolution where he had found it upon his assumption of office in 1933. But ten million Americans remained unemployed. American industry and commerce were on dead center. There were many voices, including some in the entourage of the president himself, who believed and preached that the growth of America was over, that the economic pie would never get any bigger, and that the real question facing the country was how and between what groups the existing pie should be divided.

The leading candidates in the Republican party in that winter and spring were Thomas E. Dewey, Robert A. Taft, and Arthur Vandenberg. Dewey, the thirty-eight-year-old district attorney of New York County, who had made a reputation as a racket buster in the Empire State and whose experience in national and international affairs was wholly

17

untested, was ambivalent on the subject of the war. He was neither an interventionist nor a committed isolationist. Taft and Vandenberg, both leaders in the small Republican minority in the Senate, were committed isolationists, agreeing fully with the point of view which made it possible for President Hoover to finesse the question of the possible defeat by Germany of England and France. The machinery of the Republican party was in the hands of numberless local organizations spread through the forty-eight states, some venal, almost all petty, whose dominating force, to the extent that there was any dominating force, was a hatred of "that man in the White House."

How then did Wendell Willkie become the Republican nominee? To find out what happened we must go back to April 1940, two months before the Republican convention was to meet in Philadelphia.

II

In the spring of 1940 I was twenty-eight years old, unmarried, living at home with my mother and stepfather, working as a lawyer in the great Wall Street law firm headed by John W. Davis, former congressman from West Virginia, former solicitor general of the United States, former ambassador to the Court of St. James's, and, in 1924, Democratic candidate for president. I was also a member of the New York Young Republican Club and, like many others, a surveyor of the Republican, the national, and the international scenes.

As a surveyor of those scenes, I, together with others, began to wonder how long the phony war would stay phony, whether the growth of America was indeed over, and whether having ten million unemployed was a necessary constant of our national life. Together with others, I looked at Dewey, Taft and Vandenberg, and, respecting them though I did, wondered whether they offered the answers to our problems. And I read an occasional column in the newspapers, such as several written by Arthur Krock in *The New York Times,* which indicated that the best of all presidents would be a man named Wendell Willkie. But everybody, including the writers of the columns, agreed that his nomination was obviously impossible.

Willkie's nomination was obviously impossible because Taft and Dewey and Vandenberg had a tremendous lead in delegates already chosen, and the convention was only a few weeks away. It was made even more impossible by the fact that Willkie was chief executive of a vast public utility holding company, with his office in Wall Street—the citadel of all that Roosevelt had campaigned against and defeated in 1936, only four short years before. What made it most impossible was the fact that Willkie had been an enrolled Democrat until the fall of 1939, less than a year before, and had voted for Roosevelt in the 1936 election.

But the thought would not die that if a Willkie nomination were possible—obviously it was not, but if by some miracle it just were possible—he would indeed make a great president. He was articulate, energetic, and magnetic. He believed deeply in the free enterprise system, of which he was a leader, but he was also a passionate defender of civil rights and the right to dissent. Paradoxical, unruly perhaps, but positive and constructive in his philosophy, he was withal a giant, and there were not many giants around, certainly not in the Republican party of that era.

Not only did one read in the columns in those days about Willkie's desirability, but one heard it at social occasions, both when dining with one's parents' friends and when having a drink with one's contemporaries. Willkie debated on the radio with Robert Jackson, assistant attorney general of the United States, and thereafter the suggestions of his availability grew. Willkie participated in a widely followed radio program called "Information Please," and the discussion of his possible nomination became more frequent. But always the person making the suggestion assumed its impossibility and assumed that he was alone, or, at best, part of a very small group in thinking as he did about Wendell Willkie.

So it was that in April of 1940 I decided to make a test. I decided to find out—or try to find out—whether the support for Willkie was sporadic and isolated or whether, as I believed and hoped, it was deeper and more widespread than anybody suspected. As it happened, my decision to make the test, although considered for several days, was finally arrived at over drinks with a charming lady, then young and unmarried, who is now the wife of Marquis Childs, the well-known writer.

III

The first thing I had to determine was to what group I would turn to make the test. Since I was young and relatively impecunious, there was no thought of doing a commercial poll. I finally decided to send a mailing to the Princeton class of 1924 and the Yale class of 1925. This would give some slight geographical diversity to the test, more at least than would be accomplished by taking names at random from the telephone book. The group would consist of men approximately thirty-five years old—old enough to be seriously concerned about the country and the world and yet young enough not to be too set in their thinking. Most important in the selection of that group, however, was the practical fact that as a Princeton graduate I had the

Princeton alumni directory on my desk and my office-mate, a Yale graduate, was able to produce a counterpart from Yale.

The next decision to be made was the form of the text to be mailed out. I decided to prepare a document calling for the nomination and election of Wendell Willkie, with provision for some fifteen signatures on each copy. I listed my name and residence address with the request that the documents when signed be returned to me. I also listed the name of the well-known legal printer who printed the documents so that anybody interested could purchase additional copies directly, thus saving me from further financial investment should the process turn out to be successful. I decided not to address the document to any person or body and to call it a Declaration rather than a petition. Politically inexperienced though I was, I was certainly knowledgeable enough to realize that as a practical matter the only nomination which Willkie could have was the Republican nomination. However, I thought it worthwhile to play the political ingenue to the hilt. I therefore took the position that it made no difference who nominated Willkie, just so long as he became president.

The text of the Declaration was an adaptation of an article by Willkie himself which had appeared in the April edition of *Fortune*. The Declaration read as follows:

WILLKIE for PRESIDENT

We, the undersigned people of the United States, believe that Wendell Willkie should be elected President of the United States.

After twenty years of post-war government, both Republican and Democratic, there are about 10,000,000 of us Americans who are unemployed and destitute. Hundreds of thousands have lost their homes and wander this country with no place to go. Farm tenancy has increased, and in the cities young men go about begging for the right to earn a living. For the first time in American history we have heard serious talk about classes instead of individuals. Our national debt towers over us, and our capital lies idle in the banks. As a kind of explanation of this we are told that our country has reached the limits of its growth and that the future has less to offer than the past. This, we are told, is why power has been taken from us and placed in the hands of a few planners (whom we have not elected) in Washington. This is a philosophy of defeat.

Because Wendell Willkie does not believe in this philosophy of defeat we welcome him. We call for his election as President because he has a proven belief in free enterprise, yet he can contemplate with equanimity the great changes in society which these moving times require; because he knows that business is a part of life and a way of life, and that only through businesslike government can there be economic and social profit for the people; because he has a hatred of persecution inherited from his ancestors who fled to these shores to escape the persecutions of their era; because alike on matters of taxation, foreign affairs, human welfare and other issues of the day he has displayed an insight, a candor and an absence of vindictiveness which are unique in the political theatre of our time.

But more than all else we know that Wendell Willkie will not let us down. He will not let us down because he understands some fundamental things about us. He knows that we believe in personal integrity—and he shares that belief. He knows that we have a deep and abiding faith in our country—and he shares that faith. He knows that national prosperity is more beneficial to us than sectional or occupational prosperity. He will be the defender of our power and not of the power of any institution or favored group. What Wendell Willkie believes he has written and spoken without quibble. But the essence of his political philosophy is in his heart, as it is in the hearts of us, the people of the United States.

22

WILLKIE *for* PRESIDENT

We, the undersigned people of the United States, believe that Wendell Willkie should be elected President of the United States.

After twenty years of post-war government, both Republican and Democratic, there are about 10,000,000 of us Americans who are unemployed and destitute. Hundreds of thousands have lost their homes and wander this country with no place to go. Farm tenantry has increased, and in the cities young men go about begging for the right to earn a living. For the first time in American history we have heard serious talk about *classes* instead of individuals. Our national debt towers over us, and our capital lies idle in the banks. As a kind of explanation of this we are told that the country has reached the limits of its growth and that the future has less to offer than the past. This, we are told, is why power has been taken from us and placed in the hands of a few planners (whom we have not elected) in Washington. This is a philosophy of defeat.

Because Wendell Willkie does not believe in this philosophy of defeat we welcome him. We call for his election as President because he has a proven belief in free enterprise, yet he can contemplate with equanimity the great changes in society which these moving times require; because he knows that business is a part of life and a way of life, and that only through *businesslike* government can there be economic and social profit for the people; because he has a hatred of persecution inherited from his ancestors who fled to these shores to escape the persecutions of their era; because alike on matters of taxation, foreign affairs, human welfare and the other cardinal issues of the day he has displayed an insight, a candor and an absence of vindictiveness which are unique in the political theatre of our time.

But more than all else we know that Wendell Willkie will not let us down. He will not let us down because he understands some fundamental things about us. He knows that we believe in personal integrity—and he shares that belief. He knows that we have a deep and abiding faith in our country—and he shares that faith. He knows that *national* prosperity is more beneficial to us than sectional or occupational prosperity. He will be the defender of our power, and not of the power of any institution or favored group. What Wendell Willkie believes he has written and spoken without quibble. But the essence of his political philosophy is in his heart, as it is in the hearts of us the people of the United States. .

Return this Declaration, full of signatures, to:	The purpose of this	Additional copies of this Declaration can be
OREN ROOT, Jr.	declaration is to drama-	obtained for the following prices from
455 East 57th Street	tize a demand which	PANDICK PRESS, INC.
New York City	politicians will heed.	22 Thames Street
		New York, N. Y.
		$6.00 per 100; $8.00 per 500; $12.00 per 1,000.

Name	Home Address

346

The next question which had to be faced was whether I should advise Willkie in advance of what I proposed to do. I decided not to advise him, partly because I did not wish to embarrass him with the knowledge of my plan, but mainly because I did not want to take the risk of his asking me not to make the mailing. However, simultaneously with the sending of the Declarations to the Yale and Princeton alumni, I dispatched the following letter to Willkie:

April 9, 1940

Dear Mr. Willkie:

Today I have mailed copies of the enclosed to a couple of thousand people. This is only a feeler and a small beginning of what must follow to dramatize your unquestionable availability. I did not inform you of it in advance because I wished to be able to say not only that you had not sponsored it but also that you had not even known of it.

I am a young lawyer downtown, though I thought it wise to use my home address on the Declarations. Thanks to my great-uncle, Elihu Root, I have a name which catches the political eye to some degree and I am a member of the New York Young Republican Club (which has declared for Dewey). Beyond that I am only one of the I believe millions of citizens who most ardently desire your nomination and election as President.

Aside from the colossal qualifications which you have for the Presidency, it is my off the record opinion that all other candidates in the field differ from each other only in varying degrees of unfitness. If in this crisis of civilization the Republican Party turns to some ponderous isolationist or to some crooning votegetter I say it is morally bankrupt.

I have no illusions about your being nominated in Philadelphia. I do know that if nominated you will win. And I am naive enough to believe that even the Republican politicians may see the light if enough work of the right

24

kind is done at once. I propose to contribute to that work with all the vigor and imagination at my command.

Faithfully yours,
Oren Root, Jr.

Mr. Wendell L. Willkie
20 Pine Street
New York, New York

I also sent a Declaration by hand to *The New York Times* and to the *Herald Tribune,* as well as one addressed personally to Arthur Krock. The next day stories of considerable proportions appeared in both those papers, and later the story was picked up by other papers in New York City and elsewhere. The reaction to the Declarations was immediate and overwhelming. Not only did they start coming back to me in large numbers, but, as I had hoped they would, people went on their own to the printer to obtain additional Declarations for dissemination to their acquaintances. The inquiries by telephone were so numerous that even the large switchboard at my law office was swamped, to the exclusion of the firm's proper business.

The reaction from Willkie himself came swiftly but indirectly and through an unexpected intermediary.

IV

The night after the burst of publicity caused by the sending of the Declarations, I was sitting at dinner in my mother's apartment on East 57th Street when I was called to the telephone to speak, as I was told, to Mr. Thomas W. Lamont. I assumed one of my friends was pulling my leg, since Mr. Lamont was at that time the senior partner of J. P.

Morgan & Co., and it seemed most unlikely that a man of his importance would telephone me for any reason. However, I was wrong, and it was indeed Mr. Lamont on the telephone. He told me that at that moment he was attending a dinner of the Economic Club of New York where he had talked with Willkie, who was president of the club. What had transpired between him and Willkie, apparently, was a discussion of my highly publicized activity and of the best method of stopping me. I learned later that Willkie expressed a reluctance to telephone me himself, since he feared that I was probably at best an incompetent and at worst an adventurer, with the consequent danger in either case that I would misuse his call for the sake of further publicity. When it turned out that the law firm for which I worked had Mr. Lamont's bank as one of its principal clients, it was agreed that the telephone call and the effort to stop me could come more safely from him.

Complimented as I was by the call from a man of Mr. Lamont's stature, I expressed a reluctance to desist from my efforts. I was, after all, a citizen of a free country and I did in fact believe that the country's welfare would best be served by Willkie's nomination. Seeing that he alone could not convince me, and having concluded apparently that I was at least susceptible to a reasonable telephone conversation, Mr. Lamont put Willkie on the wire to assert for himself his unhappiness with my activities. When even his persuasions failed, Willkie asked me if I would be willing to meet with Russell Davenport, at that time the managing editor of *Fortune*, and, as I later learned, a close associate of Willkie. The prospect of meeting so eminent a gentleman was exciting to me, and I agreed to await Davenport's call. Davenport's assignment, of course, was to accomplish in person a termination of my efforts, where telephonic persuasions by others had proved unsuccessful.

V

One wonders why Willkie was so disturbed by what I had done. Partly, no doubt, it was for the reasons already stated, that I was unknown and therefore probably unreliable. However, the principal reason, as I later learned, was that Willkie had his own ideas about how best to obtain the Republican nomination, and my unauthorized publicity was seriously threatening a strategy which had been carefully thought out and had been in process for many months.

The principal architect of that strategy was Willkie himself. Other participants included Russell Davenport and his wife, Marcia; a publicist, Charlton McVeigh; and Harold E. Talbott, a financier. This group had been meeting at regular intervals, usually in the Davenport apartment in Manhattan, to advance the strategy of a Willkie nomination. The plan upon which they had agreed was to give Willkie as much publicity as possible in fields of public concern unrelated to the nominating process itself, in the hope that the convention would ultimately deadlock among the leading candidates and, thus deadlocked, would turn to Willkie as a dark horse. The *Fortune* article and the "Information Please" appearance were part of the plan, together with a number of other appearances by Willkie on public platforms and in print.

The basic essential of the strategy was that it be low key. Above all, there was never, never to be any mention of the true objective, the Republican nomination. The Willkie name and the Willkie philosophy were to be publicized, but not in terms of the political process and certainly not in any way to arouse the resentment of those who, in the event of a deadlocked convention, would hopefully turn to him as a compromise.

The course of action being pursued by Willkie and those

around him was not regarded by them as lacking in candor, nor in fact was it so. Partly, it was simply the latest example of an often applied method in American politics, that of the "non-candidacy." Mostly, however, it arose out of the fact that Willkie, while definitely receptive to the nomination, believed his chances of achieving it were not great. Accordingly, he did not wish to look foolish and to compromise his leadership in the area of ideas and policy, which mattered to him very much, by an open and overt campaign for the nomination.

Clearly, therefore, front-page publicity pointing precisely at the nomination, especially when it was directed by an unknown and inexperienced twenty-eight-year-old youth, was precisely what the strategists did not want. It was no wonder, then, that the effort was made to stop me.

VI

Thus it was that on the morning following my telephone conversation with Mr. Lamont and Willkie I received a call from Russell Davenport asking me to meet him under the clock at the Biltmore Hotel for lunch. It was a delightful lunch, because Russell Davenport was altogether a delightful man. We ate, we drank wine, and talked for two hours and a half. The upshot was that Davenport was convinced that my effort should continue and undertook to arrange a meeting with Willkie himself to that end.

Willkie enjoyed breakfast meetings, a practice which, perhaps because of my half-European background, has always seemed to me highly uncivilized. In any case, he and Davenport and I met for breakfast at the University Club on Fifth Avenue. I came armed with a draft of a press release saying I had met with him and that he "would not disapprove my action, though he could not approve it." Willkie changed the quoted phrase to read "would not approve nor disapprove," and he added in his own handwriting the words (referring to my efforts to obtain the nomination for him) "and that he [Willkie] would not participate in any organized move to that end." Beyond that the draft was cleared, the release went out, and to all intents and purposes the Willkie Clubs were launched. All this was done in mid-April, two short months before the convention.

VII

Here an amusing but perhaps significant personal experience should be related. It has to do with my situation in the law firm where I was employed. It started on a Friday evening when one of my young colleagues in the office telephoned to say that some of the partners were becoming increasingly upset by the dislocations which I was causing in their firm and that there was a plan afoot to confront me on Monday morning with the choice of either resigning my job or desisting from my political efforts. There was one partner in particular, so I was told, who was taking the lead in this connection (not, I need hardly say, Mr. Davis).

The news was very unsettling. I did not want to stop my Willkie activity. On the other hand, neither did I want to be fired, since the Willkie campaign would at best be an interlude in my life, and my law career was what mattered to me. So it was that I remembered Mr. Thomas W. Lamont and the telephone call which I had received from him a number of evenings earlier.

When I reached Mr. Lamont on the telephone at his house in New Jersey that Friday evening, I told him that I was confronted with a personal crisis of some magnitude and wondered, in the light of his earlier intervention in my situation, if he would be willing to see me over the weekend. Gracious gentleman that he was, he replied that his weekend was filled with house guests and visitors, but that if I would come at four o'clock on Sunday, he would see me briefly. I borrowed my family's car and arrived on the dot of four to find Mr. Lamont as good as his word. I told him of the danger which I faced in my law firm and said that I had come for his help.

At first Mr. Lamont took the position that I was greatly exaggerating his influence and that surely there was nothing he could do to be of assistance. I was finally able to persuade him, however, that a telephone call to the vociferous partner from the senior partner of Morgan & Co. simply saying a good word about me and my Willkie efforts could be critical. He agreed to make the call the following morning, and as I left I urged him to be sure to make it before 9:45. Unless the call were made by then it might have come too late, since that would be the latest that I could decently get to the office.

Ordinarily, I find it hard to be on time for work. However, that Monday morning the perversities of life brought me to the Wall Street subway exit at 9:35, ten full minutes before Mr. Lamont's deadline. So for fifteen interminable minutes (allowing a small margin for error), I sat on a bench in Trinity Church Grave Yard watching the clock and waiting for the moment when I must confront my fate.

As I entered the law firm and passed the office of the vociferous partner, I asked his secretary whether Mr. Lamont had called. The reply being in the affirmative, I asked whether the partner had spoken with Mr. Lamont. Again the answer was yes. Feeling somewhat more relaxed, I sought out my own little corner a few doors down the hall. It was some ten minutes later that the partner came bursting into my room with "Well, Oren, my boy, how is the great politician feeling today? You are doing a wonderful job. Keep it up."

I cannot remember whether I ever reported this happy result to Mr. Lamont. I hope I did because it may just be that he made a significant contribution to history on that Monday morning. Except for him, I might have had to drop my effort. Perhaps the course of events leading to Willkie's nomination would have continued unchanged even so, but considering all the forces which had to coincide during the next few weeks to bring that nomination about, I am truly glad that the call was made.

As it turned out, I soon left the law office anyway, but with a friendly "leave of absence." The situation there became impossible from both sides, and I moved to small and unpretentious quarters on Madison Avenue near Sixtieth Street, where a group of enthusiastic volunteers began to form. The partners in the law firm remained my good friends and many of them gave me strong support as the campaign progressed.

VIII

So far as my personal efforts were concerned, the campaign was almost exclusively amateur, ingenuous, and young. As a matter of fact, when I turned twenty-nine on June 13 and we had a little staff party in my windowless office in mid-Manhatattan, one of my associates was heard to say, "What a public relations disaster it would be if you were thirty."

There was, however, an occasional word of encouragement from more experienced sources. One such came in a letter from Senator Harry F. Byrd, the distinguished Democratic senior senator from Virginia, congratulating me on my effort and prophesying a Willkie nomination. My family had known Byrd well for many years and his son, Harry, Jr., who presently occupies his father's seat in the Senate, had been one of my fraternity brothers at the University of Virginia, where I attended law school.

Senator Byrd's interest in the Willkie campaign arose from many sources, not the least of which, no doubt, was his increasing disaffection with the policies of President Roosevelt. However, the senator may also have been attracted by the Willkie strategy of hoping to come from behind in a deadlocked convention, because eight years before he had pursued that same strategy at his party's convention, but in his case without success.

In the main, however, the support for Willkie grew at the grass roots. Willkie Clubs sprang up like mushrooms on a summer night. Almost without exception they were self-inspired, self-directed, and self-financed. They manufactured their own buttons, and never in the history of political campaigns have there been so many diverse types of buttons. They caused their own Declarations to be printed and in many cases arranged for the documents to be returned to local club headquarters instead of to me. In some few cases they even changed the phrases of the Declaration which I had borrowed from Willkie's *Fortune* text. From New York we tried to direct them, we tried to help them, but most of all we tried to inspire them and to urge them on.

In the Willkie camp, however, a kind of ambivalence continued to prevail. In spite of Willkie's consent to my efforts, and in spite of the warm personal relationship which existed between Davenport and me, there remained a lurking resentment in some quarters against the "crudity and garishness" of my activities. Until very late in the spring, Willkie continued to maintain the fiction that he was not seeking the nomination, and Davenport and some of those around him could not help but feel that the Willkie Club efforts, direct and unequivocal as they were, were inconsistent with the leader's posture.

Accordingly, a rival group was set up for the purpose of offsetting my efforts. The location selected for the rival headquarters was the Murray Hill Hotel, a Victorian ark located on lower Park Avenue. Nowhere in New York could quarters less inspiring have been found, and this was not accidental but deliberate.

To counteract the razzle-dazzle of the Willkie Clubs, the new group was given the sedate title Volunteer Mailing Committee for Distributing Willkie's Speeches. A press conference was held at which it was stated that the new effort was in no way directed against the old one, but the implication was clearly given that the new group was more consistent with Willkie's personal strategy than the Root activities. Unfortunately—or rather fortunately—nobody paid much attention to the Murray Hill goings on, nor did they in any material way mar the essential unity of those of us, Davenport and his associates included, who were supporting the Willkie candidacy.

IX

There was, however, one additional concern about the effort which I spearheaded. It was bad enough, some people said, for Willkie to be a utilities executive from Wall Street, but to have the leading public supporter of his cause be a Wall Street lawyer from the law firm which represented the House of Morgan simply made matters worse. How much better it would be, these people said, if the public leadership for Willkie were to come from some other part of the country than the seat of financial power.

Seeing some merit in this analysis, I decided to take action. I was not prepared to abandon or diminish my own efforts. However, I saw no reason why a similar undertaking could not "spontaneously" erupt in some more pristine locality than New York City, thus effecting a counterweight of sorts to the Wall Street effort. I consulted with Davenport, and between us we decided that the ideal locus for the new effort would be Oscaloosa, Iowa. Whether Davenport had ever been there or whether he simply plucked the name from his poetic imagination I do not know. In any case, the die was cast and on a sunny day in early May I set out for the corn belt. Since Oscaloosa at the time was a very small city, I was fearful that my registration at a local hotel might attract undue attention, thus spoiling the spontaneity of the result which I hoped would ensue. Accordingly, I spent the night in Ottumwa, a somewhat larger city nearby, and arrived in the town square of Oscaloosa by bus at 7:30 the following morning. After a cup of coffee at a local counter, I inquired from a friendly newspaperman whether he knew the name of any young lawyer in town who might be interested in an unusual political adventure. He suggested that I call upon Charles A. Williams, Jr., who he thought might fit my requirements.

Lawyers arrive in their offices earlier in Oscaloosa than they do in New York City, so I was able to find Charlie Williams before too much more time passed. Having sounded him out delicately as to his political preferences and finding that his enthusiasm for Willkie was keen and natural, I told him the whole story quite frankly, including the purpose of my visit. He liked the idea. As a matter of fact he adopted it wholeheartedly. Before the morning was over, we had planned the details and written the release for the papers. That afternoon, Charlie Williams and his charming wife took me as their guest to the Drake Relays, a much attended

34

track event in that region of the country. That night I boarded the train back to New York. Two days later, on May 4, there developed from Oscaloosa, Iowa—entirely spontaneously—a new One Man Campaign for Wendell Willkie for President. Thus the Willkie Clubs, which until that time had been concentrated to a considerable degree in the eastern part of the country, began to sprout in the heartland as well.

X

While the Willkie Clubs and their related activities were major factors in building support for the nomination, there were many other significant forces at work. Important among the other forces was the support which developed for Willkie in the press and in various influential periodicals. An eleven-page spread in the May 13 issue of *Life* gave his candidacy a big boost, and the support of widely syndicated columnists, such as Dorothy Thompson and Raymond Clapper, was also a significant element in the pre-convention buildup. Beyond that, editorial support appeared in numerous papers across the country, climaxed by a front-page editorial in the *Herald Tribune* on the day the balloting started at the Philadelphia convention.

There also developed during this period the beginnings of professional political support. Samuel F. Pryor, Jr., national committeeman from Connecticut, joined the Willkie entourage at a relatively early date, first behind the scenes, but later more openly. Other professionals were Sinclair Weeks, national committeeman from Massachusetts, and William H. Vanderbilt, the young governor of Rhode Island. These three men were important advisors in a group where they were almost the only members who had enough experience to know the mechanics of the convention process. At the very last minute Harold Stassen, the thirty-three-year-old governor of Minnesota, who was also the Keynoter of the convention, agreed to be Willkie's floor manager, and Charles Halleck, a young member of the House of Representatives from Indiana, agreed to put him in nomination.

Willkie's early associates also continued to play important and significant roles during the weeks before the convention. Harold Talbott, the financier, was the principal raiser of funds. While the nature of the campaign was such that only limited funds were required, there was obviously a need for some money, and Harold Talbott was the central figure in that regard. The most significant personality in the group around Willkie, however, was Russell Davenport. To the extent that Davenport assisted Willkie in the formulation of some of his most important public statements, it could almost be said that he was the primary creator of the Willkie image. His philosophy and Willkie's philosophy were thoroughly sympathetic, and in many circumstances it was hard to know where the thinking of one left off and the thinking of the other began.

Most important of all, however, in developing the upsurge of popular support during those pre-convention weeks, was Willkie himself. Willkie Clubs, other amateurs, speech writers, professional advisors, all these were secondary to the candidate himself, to his charisma, to his intellect, and to his shrewd if untutored political instinct. Thus, in late April Willkie addressed the annual dinner of the Bureau of Advertising of the American Newspaper Publishers Association in the Waldorf-Astoria Hotel. At the invitation of John and Gardner Cowles, publishers of influential newspapers in Minnesota and Iowa, he made an especially effective talk in St. Paul in mid-May, after which the posture of not being a candidate became increasingly difficult to maintain. Later in

May he spoke at a rally in Manhattan Center organized by a group of supporters from Indiana, the state from which he had come to New York a number of years before. At that rally I was one of the supporting speakers. On June 12 just twelve days before the convention opened, Willkie formally announced in Washington, D.C., that he was a candidate for president.

XI

So much has been written by others about the convention itself that there is no need here to rehearse in detail the chronology of events which took place on those exciting days. I would rather give a few impressions as seen from my personal vantage point, fully realizing that the part I saw was only a fraction of the whole.

One of the most significant factors, it seems to me, is that when Willkie arrived in Philadelphia on June 22, two days before the formal opening of the convention, he had no firm delegates at all. All the delegates were either already committed to one or another of the leading candidates or they were uncommitted. Willkie's task was to do what no candidate in modern times in either party had ever done: to develop his basic strength by the conversion at the convention itself of delegates previously committed to others. He accomplished this in a number of ways, but primarily by the force of his own personality. The circumstances in which that personality was functioning in Philadelphia that last week of June included the appointment a few days before by President Roosevelt of two famous Republicans, Henry L. Stimson and Frank Knox, to his cabinet, thus creating at least the facade of coalition government, and the ominous events transpiring on the battlefields of Europe. The times clearly called for greatness, and nobody was more ready to answer the call than Wendell L. Willkie.

Headquarters arrangements at the convention had been made by all the leading candidates long in advance. Senator Taft had over a hundred rooms in one hotel; District Attorney Dewey had over seventy rooms in another; and other candidates, including a number of favorite sons, had suites appropriate to their aspirations. By the time that it was decided to seek space for Willkie and his entourage, substantially all the desirable space had already been committed. By virtue of the efforts of William H. Harman, who was chairman of the Willkie Clubs of Pennsylvania, a modest suite of rooms was obtained in the Land Title Building, and this functioned as the principal Willkie headquarters. In addition, Harman had procured a store front on Broad Street which functioned, under my general guidance, as the gathering place for the thousands of amateurs who came to Philadelphia to help. Willkie himself, with his charming wife Edith, occupied a suite of only two small rooms in the Benjamin Franklin Hotel.

The leading candidates remained very much behind the scenes, plotting their strategy in staff meetings and by telephone, and appearing publicly only from time to time for formal press conferences. Willkie's method was entirely different. Realizing that his objective was not to hold and expand his strength among the delegates, since he had none, but rather to convert to his cause delegates already committed to others, he made himself available to anybody who wished to see him. Volunteers from the street-front headquarters fanned out through the hotel lobbies and bars of the city, buttonholing delegates and bringing them to meet Willkie in his cramped Benjamin Franklin rooms. For eighteen hours a day the candidate shuttled back and forth between those two rooms, one room being filled while he was addressing the group in the other. No questions were barred, and every question got a direct reply. The effect on the delegates was electric. Not everybody agreed with all his answers, but it was a rare delegate who was not impressed by his vigor, his frankness, and the broad range of his intellect and his views.

Beyond the personal contact between Willkie and the delegates and the volunteers who had come on their own initiative and at their own expense to Philadelphia, there was a barrage of telegrams from all over the country, the magnitude of which had never before been seen in any comparable situation. Delegates returning to their rooms at night found hundreds and even thousands of telegrams awaiting them, signed in many cases by persons whose names they recognized as supporters of the Republican party back home. In a dispatch dated June 25, carrying the by-line of Emmet Crozier, a distinguished political reporter, the *Herald Tribune* reported that "the flood of mail and telegrams urging Mr. Willkie's nomination continued to amaze the politicians and confound the ranks of rival candidates. It was estimated that nearly a million messages from all parts of the country had been received here since the delegates began to assemble last Saturday."

There were some who asserted at the time that the pressure of the telegrams was doing more harm than good, that it could backfire. Personally, I never accepted that opinion. As a matter of fact, after hearing that point of view advanced with some heat by a delegate not previously friendly to our cause, my reaction was to commit a part of our remaining slender funds to a telegram to all Willkie Clubs in the nation saying "Telegrams tremendously effective. Redouble all efforts."

There was also the matter of the galleries. Relatively passive at first, the galleries became increasingly pro-Willkie as

the convention progressed. Indeed at the time of the balloting on the third day of the convention, the cries of "We
Want Willkie" that came from the galleries seemed almost
unanimous. So passionate did the galleries become that there
were periods during the convention when the pro-Willkie
galleries and the pro-Taft and pro-Dewey delegates on the
floor were booing each other from different sections of the
hall.

How the galleries became so heavily pro-Willkie is still
disputed. Some people have advanced the theory that they
were somehow illegally packed. The only light which I can
shed upon the situation arises from my personal experience.
If the galleries were to have been packed, the logical people
with whom to have packed them were the amateurs and
volunteers who worked out of the Broad Street store front
which I operated. The fact is that fifty seats were assigned
to that store front in a gallery holding several thousand.

I have no doubt that ingenious and enthusiastic young
Willkie people did in some instances wangle their way into
the galleries without tickets. However, as I took my seat in
the gallery on the night that Willkie's name was put in nomination, I observed that the great majority of people there
were wearing Taft or Dewey insignia. This is not surprising
since the seats had been allocated many months before on
the basis of organizational support in the various states. At
the time of the allocation of the seats, Willkie not only had
no organizational support but was not even an avowed candidate, so no seats at all had been allocated to him. The few
seats that were ultimately allocated to Willkie were scraped
together at the last moment after the strength of his candidacy became apparent. What happened in the galleries, I am
convinced, is that individuals who had obtained their seats
through the organizations supporting Taft, Dewey, and
other leading candidates, were themselves swept away by

the Willkie spirit and were converted to his cause during the course of the convention itself.

There were many critical moments as the balloting progressed. Willkie's surprising 105 votes on the first ballot gave him an even stronger start than most of his supporters expected. The polling of the New York delegation in the third ballot, during which Dewey's strength, already diminishing, was further eroded by Willkie in Dewey's home state, was of great psychological importance. Willkie's move into first place on the fourth ballot, with 306 votes to 254 for Taft and 250 for Dewey, was perhaps decisive.

However, the result might well have been different had it not been for the decision of Joseph W. Martin, permanent chairman of the convention, not to adjourn the convention at the end of the fifth ballot. On that ballot both Willkie and Taft had moved up, mostly at the expense of Dewey, who was fading rapidly. When Senator Taft's supporters saw the result of that ballot, they decided to seek an adjournment until the next day. If all the votes scattered among Senator Vandenberg, Governor James of Pennsylvania, former President Hoover, and others could be moved into Taft's column, Willkie could still be stopped and Taft could be nominated. Since most of the delegates supporting those other candidates were conservative in their outlook, the possibility of consolidating them behind the Ohio senator seemed very real. An adjournment would provide the time to take the necessary steps, and a motion to that effect was made.

There had been a recess for dinner, and the third ballot had not started until after 8:30 in the evening. By the time the fifth ballot was over and the motion to adjourn was made, the hour was after midnight. There was ample justification for Chairman Martin to grant the motion, or at least to put it to a vote. Martin, the minority leader of the House of Representatives, was an organization politician of long standing and basically conservative. Many believed that he would be sympathetic to the motion to adjourn. That he was not may have been due to his New England sense of his duty as presiding officer, or perhaps to some instinct which told him that to try to stem the Willkie tide at that late moment by a technical maneuver could spell ruin for the party. In any case, he ruled the motion out of order and, at his direction, the roll call for the sixth and final ballot began.

It was nearly two o'clock in the morning when Governor Bricker of Ohio, Senator Taft's leading supporter, moved to make the nomination of Wendell Willkie unanimous. The galleries, which had been growing wilder as the night progressed, exploded in cheers, and across the country millions of people glued to their radios knew that they had heard one of the great political dramas of modern times.

XII

The question which continues to be asked about the Willkie nomination is whether it resulted from a genuine and spontaneous grass roots effort or whether it was contrived by powerful financial and publishing interests which, while preserving the appearances of spontaneity, in fact gave it central direction. Those in a position to have opinions have expressed their views on both sides of this question. I can do no more than express mine from what I experienced and what I saw. In my view, the answer lies somewhere in between the two extremes, but with the spontaneous aspect far outweighing any organized direction from any source.

The reason why the question is so often raised, it seems to me, is that the nomination was brought about by a coincidence of a multitude of factors, the absence of any of which would probably have changed the result. Because of that, there is a normal tendency to look for some contrived and carefully directed force behind the scenes. In my opinion not only was there no such behind-the scenes direction, at least not in any sense which by itself determined the result, but the factors which resulted in the nomination were so diverse, so complex, and so massive in their accumulated effect that no central direction could possibly have brought them about. The nomination has sometimes been referred to as a political miracle. That, it seems to me, is exactly what it was. Writing in *The New York Times* from Philadelphia on June 23, Arthur Krock reported: "From so many directions has this movement converged on Philadelphia and so active and various in classification are its members, that workers for the other candidates have been wondering aloud whether some remarkable secret organization, skilled in politics and heavily financed, has been doing spade work which is responsible. Not only is there no such organization, but until the early hours of today there was not even the basically necessary strategy board or any real move to form it."

There is no doubt that powerful financial and publishing interests were in support of the Willkie candidacy in the weeks before the convention. Leaders in those fields, together with many others in the country, were concerned about some of President Roosevelt's domestic programs and were anxious for the Republican party to nominate a candidate who could gain the White House and change them. They were particularly concerned about the New Deal philosophy that the United States had reached the end of its period of economic growth and all that was left to do was to share equally such wealth as then existed.

However, in the area of foreign policy, these same leading financiers and publicists, many of whom were involved in international activities of considerable scope, found themselves in substantial agreement with President Roosevelt's position on the war which was then underway in Europe. In the winter and spring of 1940, that position was probably best expressed by a group headed by William Allen White, editor of the *Emporia Gazette,* known as the Committee to Defend America by Aiding the Allies. The problem facing these financial and publishing leaders, therefore, was to find a candidate who had a chance to win the White House, who believed in the dynamics of the free enterprise system, but who also recognized the importance of not allowing Hitler to win the war. Willkie measured up to those requirements better than any of the more prominent candidates.

It would be foolish to deny that these leaders had some influence on pre-convention developments. As the grass roots reaction began to grow, Willkie supporters in eastern financial houses were in a position through their correspondent relationships and their wire services across the country to communicate their views rapidly and effectively and thus to fan the flames. The great magazines, such as *Life* and others, reached an audience which in the days before television would have been very difficult to reach so promptly in any other way.

None of this would have had any effect, however, if there had not been hundreds of thousands of ordinary people thoughout the country who felt substantially the same way as these leaders and who reacted positively to the possibility of Willkie's nomination, whether as a result of suggestions from others or spontaneously on their own. How many signatures were finally put on the Declarations could never be accurately determined, although the published estimate was four and a half million. The reason that it could not be accurately determined was that only a relatively small percentage were returned to me as a result of my original mailing and as a result of the mailings by others who adopted my form. Many of the Willkie Clubs provided for their Declarations to be returned directly to them. These in turn were submitted directly to the delegates from the areas where they were gathered, which was a great deal more effective than having them amassed in some central location. Even by the most conservative estimates, however, the people who procured the signatures on the Declarations and who bombarded the delegates with telegrams were far too numerous to have been the agents of any centrally directed apparatus, even assuming that such an apparatus had been in existence.

Underlying the whole movement, of course, were the tremendous events taking place in Europe in the period immediately preceding the convention. The idea that the war was phony had fallen apart when Hitler marched into the Low Countries. In England Prime Minister Chamberlain, who two years before had come back from a meeting with Hitler promising "peace in our time," had been replaced by the aggressive and dynamic Winston Churchill. Finally, on June 14, twelve days before the nominating speeches in Philadelphia, Paris fell. It was against this background that the country measured the candidacies of Taft, Dewey, and Vandenberg and found them lacking. It was against this background that Wendell Willkie, who hoped to keep the United States out of war but who knew the meaning of an allied defeat, captured the imagination of the country.

Central to the whole situation, of course, was Willkie himself. His freshness, his candor, his freedom from the restraints of an active political past—all these and other qualities made him the man of the hour and inspired the uprising from coast to coast which rolled over the established machinery of the Republican party and brought about his nomination.

XIII

As it turned out, the moment of Willkie's nomination was the high-watermark of his political career. During the ensuing campaign he made a tremendous effort. He crisscrossed the country on his campaign train and continued to pour his magnetism and his physical and intellectual energy into the struggle. His principal emphasis was opposition to Roosevelt's desire for a third term, which shattered the two-term tradition going back to President Washington, and his deep belief in the productive processes of the United States. Over and over again he repeated the phrase "Only the productive can be strong and only the strong can be free."

But the running of a nationwide campaign proved more difficult than capturing a convention. The very manner of Willkie's nomination resulted in his not having an effective organization ready for the campaign itself. As the effort began to flounder during the summer, criticisms came in from all sides. There were some who said that he relied too heavily on inexperienced amateurs and ignored the regular party apparatus. There were others who asserted that he allowed himself to become a captive of the regulars and had abandoned the enthusiastic volunteers who had nominated him.

Neither of these accusations was true. The fact is that Willkie did his best to combine the enthusiasm of the amateurs with the experience of the regulars. He appointed Joseph W. Martin, the minority leader of the House of Representatives, chairman of the Republican National Committee, from which post he became the manager of the campaign. A constant and close advisor on the train was Henry Cabot Lodge, at the time a young and vigorous senator from Massachusetts. Samuel Pryor was designated eastern campaign manager and Sinclair Weeks, another experienced professional, continued to play a significant role. On the other hand, Russell Davenport, the original amateur, remained close to the candidate and was designated his personal representative. Likewise, the Willkie Clubs continued, and through their efforts tens of thousands of people were introduced to the political process for the first time.

Willkie wanted very much to win. But even at the height of the campaign he remembered that the welfare of the country came ahead of personal victory. Thus, when the president sent feelers inquiring what Willkie's reaction would be if an arrangement were to be made to supply fifty over-aged destroyers to England in return for certain military bases, some permanent and some on lease, Willkie replied that he would not make an issue of it. When the announcement of the famous "destroyer deal" was made, Willkie was as good as his word. In retrospect one can see in this action a forerunner of his later support of Roosevelt in the post-election months.

Roosevelt's strategy at first was to refrain from campaigning openly on the theory that the best campaign was to continue to function as president. As the Willkie effort began to gain ground in the late summer and early fall, however, Roosevelt changed his strategy and made a number of political appearances with great effect. In this connection, an interesting footnote to history occurred.

One day during the winter of 1941, a number of months after the election, Russell Davenport, a strong supporter of the allied cause, received a telephone call from Harry Hopkins, one of Roosevelt's closest advisors, inviting him to the White House to meet the president. Davenport was thrilled by the invitation, believing and hoping that the president would seek his help in some aspect of the war effort. Upon arrival at the White House he was taken by Hopkins to an upstairs sitting room where a number of the president's close confidants were gathered awaiting Roosevelt's arrival. In due course the president was wheeled into the room. After mixing his favorite cocktail and chatting briefly with some of those present, he turned to Davenport. "Ah, Mr. Davenport," he said, "I am pleased to meet you. You and your friend, Wendell Willkie, waged a much more effective campaign than I expected. As a matter of fact, it was so effective that you upset all my plans. I had to abandon my policy of keeping quiet and go out and make a series of speeches. If I hadn't, you might have won." At that there was an appropriate ripple of laughter through the room and the president departed. Hopkins and Davenport dined alone in Hopkins's private suite. That was the end of the story so far as Roosevelt and Davenport were concerned, and Davenport never learned whether the president had had something to suggest and changed his mind, or whether he had just wanted an opportunity to meet him and to gloat over the election victory.

XIV

On election eve, Willkie made a number of final radio appearances. It was my privilege to appear with him on one of them. As we awaited the signal to go on the air, he said to me, "I think we have a real chance. I believe there will be a big silent vote." Both of us knew that when one has to count on a silent vote the chances of victory are not too good.

Although he lost the election, Willkie's twenty-two million votes were the largest number ever given to a Republican candidate up to that time. In his Loyal Opposition radio talk on Armistice Day, six days after his defeat, he laid the groundwork for the support which he later gave to the administration in the difficult months preceding Pearl Harbor.

His actions in that period disillusioned many of his earlier anti-Roosevelt supporters, but gained him new friends and new admirers in other quarters.

In 1944 Willkie tried again to capture the Republican nomination, but four years of careful organizing by Thomas E. Dewey, who was by then the governor of New York, could not be overcome. After his defeat in the Wisconsin primary that year, Willkie abandoned the race, and at the convention that summer Dewey was nominated. On October 8, 1944, Willkie died.

While Willkie failed twice in his objective of winning the presidency, in the process of those failures he made enormous contributions to the welfare of his country. And he created so indelible an impression on his fellow citizens that people to this day remember the 1940 campaign when many more recent campaigns have disappeared from their memories.

CHAPTER TWO

World War II Years

I

In recent days it is fashionable in some quarters to compare the divisions within our country concerning the Vietnam War with recollections of national unity and resolve with respect to World War II. There are those today who portray the struggle against the fascist powers as one of clear principle upon which all Americans from the very beginning were fully agreed. There is also a tendency to view the anti-war sentiment of the 1960s as something entirely new in our society.

One could contradict the last assertion by going back to the anti-draft riots of the Civil War and to the dissenters from that war who were given the name Copperheads. The resistance to the Civil War draft was especially strong in New York City, where the large foreign population was unsympathetic to the Negro cause. During one riot in that city in 1863, an entire block of houses and shops was destroyed and an orphanage for black children on Fifth Avenue was burned to the ground. Martial law was declared, and before the turmoil was ended a thousand people lay dead.

But it is not necessary to go back that far to find war resistance in the United States. It was in the mid-thirties that there appeared on American campuses loosely organized groups calling themselves Veterans of Future Wars. The title was clearly ironic and intended to be so, since the philosophy of those groups was pacifist. They followed in spirit if not in detail the famous proposition debated in that same general period at the Oxford Union in England: "Resolved that this House will not fight for King and Country." During the time between the passage of selective service in 1940 and the attack at Pearl Harbor, moreover, the slogan "over the hill in October"—a phrase calling for massive desertions—was in fairly wide circulation. It would, of course, be a mistake to exaggerate the comparison between the two periods, because neither in England nor in the United States did the draft resistance during World War II ever reach the point that it did in the United States during the Vietnam War. But it is nevertheless worth remembering that the pacifist position is not exclusively a manifestation of our modern era.

There were, in addition, the deep differences among our people as to whether the war which began in Europe in 1939 involved our national interest, and we have seen some aspects of the influence of those differences upon the presidential campaign of 1940. The important distinction between World War II and the Vietnam War so far as public psychology was concerned, of course, was that once we were actually involved in the earlier war, all division ceased. Though large segments of our population may have differed with President Roosevelt's pre-Pearl Harbor moves toward increased support of the allied cause, once the Japanese attack occurred, the country was united.

Even then, however, the war was a war without élan. Where World War I had had its slogans—"make the world safe for democracy"—its marching bands, its songs—"Over There," "It's a Long Way to Tipperary," "Madelon," and others—World War II was regarded by the generation which fought it as a grim business, necessary because we were in it and had to win, but an enterprise in which one gritted one's teeth and prayed that it would soon be over. Indeed, there were editorial writers and others in those days who worried whether the American troops knew "what they were fighting for." One of the best responses to this concern was made by Bill Mauldin in *Up Front*, a compilation of his famous wartime cartoons: "We don't have to be indoctrinated or told there is a war on over here. We know there is a war on because we see it. We don't like it a damned bit, but you don't see many soldiers quitting, so fancy propaganda would be a little superfluous."

For me World War II was a very different experience than it was for Willie and Joe, the principal characters of Mauldin's cartoons. I had been for some years in the Naval Reserve and in April 1941 I was called to active duty. Perhaps because of the publicity I had received in the Willkie campaign, I was assigned to a succession of important staffs. Since this was something over which I had no control, I am neither boasting of it nor do I apologize for it. It did result in my seeing the war from a rather high level and of observing some of the personality traits of important personages. War, like peace, has many facets, and the facet of World War II which I saw, being more detailed than grand, more personal than heroic, is, together with that war's other facets, a part of history.

Everybody who was an adult at the time remembers

52

where he was on Pearl Harbor Day and how he heard the news. I heard the news at the house of Henry and Clare Luce on King Street in Greenwich, Connecticut.

Henry R. Luce, known to family and friends as Harry, was one of the most famous, dynamic, and influential men of his times. Born in Tengchow, China, the son of a Protestant missionary, he later went to Hotchkiss School and Yale. His mother was Elizabeth Middleton Root, the daughter of a Utica, New York, lawyer. Through his mother he and I were distantly related, a fact of which I always was and am proud. Following the founding in 1923 of *Time,* the weekly news magazine, he built a career in journalism which put him at the very summit of that profession until the day of his death more than forty years later. Insofar as publicists played a role in the meteoric rise of Wendell Willkie, he was one of the leaders. His wife, Clare Boothe, combined great beauty and intellectual power into a career of variety and distinction. Starting as a magazine editor, she went on to become a playwright. *The Women, Kiss the Boys Goodbye,* and *Margin for Error* were the best known of her plays. Later she served two terms in the House of Representatives as well as a tour of duty as our ambassador in Rome. During the Willkie campaign she engaged in a highly publicized rebuttal at Carnegie Hall directed toward Dorothy Thompson, the columnist, who although an early supporter of Willkie, had at the last moment shifted to Roosevelt.

Harry and Clare's house in Greenwich was the center of one of the liveliest groups of writers, politicians, theater people, businessmen, and other leaders in the whole country. An invitation for dinner or, better still, for the weekend, was rarely turned down. I had the good fortune from time to time during the spring and summer of 1941 to receive such an invitation, and even now I look back upon those experiences with excitement and appreciation.

On Sunday, December 7, 1941, a young lawyer friend of

mine and I were luncheon guests at the home of Mr. and
Mrs. Basil Harris in Rye, New York. As we started back to
New York City after lunch, I suggested that we drop by for
a brief call on Harry and Clare Luce. As we walked into
their living room, Clare said, "How is it that you are not in
uniform?" I replied that she well knew that because we were
not at war we were not required to wear a uniform off duty.
"But," she said, "we are at war. The Japanese have attacked
Pearl Harbor." She then introduced us to her other guests,
who included Lin Yutang, the noted Chinese philosopher,
and Vincent Sheean, the well-known writer, who had passed
a substantial time in the Orient. Harry Luce himself, having
been born in China of missionary parents, was also something of an expert on Far Eastern affairs. If one were to have
designed the circumstances in which to hear the portentous
news, one could hardly have designed them more dramatically. There was, of course, a lively discussion. So sudden
and surprising was the news that even the experts present
were at that moment unable to assess the consequences. But
for Harry Luce both the event and the China orientation of
his guests on that occasion had special significance. Partly
because of his background, but also because of his study of
history, he had long been convinced that the United States
was greatly underestimating both the Japanese military
threat and its own destiny as a Pacific power. He had
pressed this view on President Roosevelt at a number of personal meetings, but had always come away feeling that his
views had not gotten through. The attack on Pearl Harbor,
terrible as it was, was therefore for him a kind of vindica-
tion.

I saw a good deal of the Luces in those days, and a fort-
night later, when I had the pleasure of taking Clare to lunch,
I brought up the subject of Monsignor Fulton J. Sheen, who
was at the time one of the most effective and well-known

preachers in the Catholic Church but whom she had never met. She expressed an interest in hearing him, and I agreed to arrange for us to attend midnight mass on Christmas Eve at the Blessed Sacrament Church on the west side of Manhattan, where Monsignor Sheen was scheduled to preach.

Having made the commitment, I then began to get cold feet. Clare's first marriage had terminated in divorce, and the Catholic Church was less tolerant of such circumstances in those times than it is today. While obviously anybody could walk in and attend mass, midnight mass with Monsignor Sheen preaching would be so crowded that either one would have to get there two hours in advance, which I hesitated to ask Clare to do, or one would have to make special arrangements. My cold feet arose out of a question as to what would be the reaction of the pastor of the Blessed Sacrament Church if I were to seek such special arrangements for a divorced woman.

As it turned out, my fears were wholly groundless. In response to my inquiry as to whether seats could be reserved for Mrs. Henry R. Luce and me, the genial pastor responded, "Could that be Clare Luce, the playwright, that you want to bring, Oren? What a pleasure it would be to look down from the pulpit upon such a beautiful woman. Of course, I will reserve the seats."

When I called for Clare that evening in her apartment in the Waldorf-Astoria Towers, Harry Luce said that he would like to come with us. Harry was a man of deep religious conviction who could talk as readily on such subjects as the writings of Teilhard de Chardin, the Jesuit evolutionist, as on the subjects of politics or international relations. Monsignor Sheen's sermon that night was a particularly effective one on the subject of human love as compared to divine love. Because it was only two weeks after Pearl Harbor, the mass concluded with the singing of "The Star-Spangled Banner."

All in all, it was a dramatic occasion. It was only a few years thereafter that Clare Luce was received into the Catholic Church by Monsignor Sheen. There are some who have suggested that Harry Luce was unhappy about his wife's conversion. I know this not to be true. While of course he had reservations about her decision, he was at all times fully supportive of her action in this respect.

II

In January 1942 I was transferred to the Navy Department in Washington, D.C. Life in wartime Washington for an unmarried young naval officer was almost embarrassingly pleasant. In both of my tours of duty there, the first one in 1942 and the second in late 1944 and 1945, I lived in comfortable houses with a group of other bachelor officers of about my age. The second house, on Chain Bridge Road, belonged to Eleanor Lansing Dulles, a sister of John Foster Dulles and Allen Dulles, and a lady of distinction in her own right. We entertained easily and frequently, had a maid to do our cooking and housework, and simply divided the cost of running the house at the end of each month. My best recollection is that the per person cost for all that came to the incredibly modest sum of about $150 per month, everything included, which was well within the boundaries of our military pay.

In 1942 Henry Wallace was the vice president of the United States. Wallace was a highly controversial figure and, while I did not agree with many of his views, I was interested in his mystique and hoped he would appear at one of the parties to which, perhaps because of the notoriety I had gained in the Willkie effort, I was from time to time invited. In the light of his shy and retiring personality, however, I should have known that a cocktail party would be the last place to look for him. As it turned out, I met him in much more informal circumstances. I was sitting on a bench awaiting my turn to play tennis at the tennis courts of the Wardman-Park Hotel when another waiting player sat down beside me. It was the vice president of the United States.

Later on, I came to know Henry Wallace moderately well. We played tennis occasionally and then, on my second tour of duty in Washington in 1945, I had the opportunity of visiting his house with his daughter Jean. Jean was engaged to and later married Leslie Douglas, who was one of the group of young officers with whom I was living.

Controversial though he was in his public life, Henry Wallace was a quiet and studious gentleman in private. After the war, he retired to a large farm in South Salem, New York, where I had occasion to visit him periodically until his death. His interest in experimental farming was very great, and in later years it was much easier to get him into a discussion on that subject than it was to have a conversation on politics or public affairs. I always found it hard to understand how he decided to become the candidate of the Progressive party in the 1948 presidential election, thus allowing himself to be used as the instrument of the extreme left and thereby splitting the Democratic party to which he owed so much.

Of the many social experiences which I had in Washington, two in particular stand out. Both occurred in my second tour of Washington duty. The first involved Mrs. Roosevelt, the wife of the president. While it is not an important story, it so clearly emphasizes that very great lady's simplicity and humility that perhaps it tells more about her than some other more widely publicized episodes.

As I was leaving my post in the South Atlantic, where I served during 1943, a young officer, Ensign James Lanigan, who was a friend of Mrs. Roosevelt, urged me to telephone her upon my return to Washington. It seemed to me a highly presumptuous thing for a person of my position and junior rank to telephone the wife of the Commander in Chief. However, Jim Lanigan insisted that Mrs. Roosevelt would be happy to hear from any friend of his. Accordingly, one morning following my return to Washington, I lifted the telephone at my inconspicuous desk in the Navy Department, called the White House, and asked for Mrs. Roosevelt. I explained to a secretary the occasion of my call and was told that the message would be repeated to Mrs. Roosevelt. That same afternoon, the secretary called back to inquire whether I could dine with Mrs. Roosevelt at the White House that evening.

The invitation put me in a terrible quandary. Naturally, I was enormously complimented by it and wanted very much to accept. I was also aware of the unwritten rule that one never turns down an invitation to the White House. On the other hand, Constantine and Marcella Mittendorf had invited me to dinner that same evening and I had already said that I would come. Connie Mittendorf was a young naval officer who had been one of the group with which I had lived during my first Washington duty. He and his wife, Marcella, had arranged the party that evening especially for me and had invited a number of our mutual friends to gather for the purpose of seeing me. At the very moment I was receiving the invitation from the White House, I knew that Marcella was working over a hot stove preparing the dinner. What should I do? Where did my duty lie?

I resolved my dilemma by taking my courage in my hands and telling the secretary the truth. I said that I hoped Mrs. Roosevelt would forgive me, but that I could not let my young friends down. As I hung up the telephone, I was seized with fear as to the consequences of what I had done.

But that was because I had underestimated Mrs. Roosevelt's generosity and human kindness. An hour later the White House secretary was back on the telephone to say that Mrs. Roosevelt fully understood, and could I come to tea the following afternoon. Needless to say, I accepted with alacrity and had an altogether delightful hour with a great and understanding lady. In post-war years I had the opportunity to serve with Mrs. Roosevelt on a number of committees in New York, and I never ceased to marvel at the very qualities which I had encountered in this first meeting.

The other Washington social occasion which I well remember was a dinner at Decatur House, the beautiful and historic residence of Mrs. Truxton Beale on Lafayette Place, now a museum. I was invited for Sunday evening at seven o'clock. Since I did not know Mrs. Beale very well, I assumed that it must be a large party and that it would not be necessary to arrive at exactly the time for which I was invited. I had difficulty in getting a taxi, however, and instead of arriving at fifteen minutes or so after seven, as I had planned, I did not arrive until some forty minutes after the appointed hour. Far from being a large party, it turned out to be a dinner for twelve, with Secretary of the Navy Forrestal as the guest of honor. My deep embarrassment was a consequence not only of my social gaffe but also of my admiration for the secretary. Together with men like Stimson and Lovett and McCloy, he had come to Washington from the world of New York finance and law. Like them, he brought to his work a sense of public service and devotion for which his countrymen should be ever grateful. To have offended him was as great an offense as to have offended my hostess.

Fortunately, so far as the secretary was concerned, however, my bad manners were not of sufficient moment to block an episode which occurred a number of months later.

The war had ended, both in the Atlantic and in the Pacific, and I had been advised that I would be released from active duty in December 1945. A few weeks before that date, as I was sitting at my desk in the Navy Department, I received word that the secretary would like to see me. This being a very unusual summons, I repaired to his office with mixed feelings of anticipation and foreboding. He was too busy to see me at once, and we ended by talking in his official car on the way to an outside appointment.

This was the period during which the proposed unification of the armed forces was under consideration. The secretary told me that, while he accepted many aspects of unification in principle, he had grave reservations about some of the specific proposals which were then being advanced. He wondered what my views were and whether I might be willing to extend my period of active duty to help him with some of the details of the proposed legislation.

Needless to say, I was enormously complimented by the request. However, I had been on active duty for nearly five years and had already made plans for my return to civilian life. More importantly, I was so firm a believer in unification of the armed forces that I had considerable question as to whether I could be of constructive help in the situation, and I told him so frankly. The secretary, of course, had the power to order me to stay. James Forrestal was not that kind of man, however, and I returned to inactive duty on schedule. In 1947 the armed forces were in fact unified and Forrestal was appointed to the new cabinet position of secretary of defense, from which post he initiated a comprehensive reorganization and coordination of the groups under his jurisdiction. He resigned in 1949, suffering from what Navy doctors called "a severe depression of the type seen in operational fatigue during the war," and a few months later

the world was shocked by the news of his death by a fall
from a window of the Navy hospital at Bethesda, Maryland.

III

Pleasant as life was in wartime Washington in 1942, I was
happy when orders came through late in the year transferring me to the staff of Vice Admiral Jonas H. Ingram, commander of the Fourth Fleet, which was situated in the South
Atlantic Ocean with headquarters in Recife, Brazil.

At that time and until the Mediterranean was opened by
the allied landings in Sicily, the South Atlantic was a strategic area of great importance. A significant part of the supplies going from the United States to the allies in Europe,
Asia, and Africa, including virtually all the supplies going to
the Red Sea as part of the buildup for the battle of El Alamein
and those going to the Persian Gulf as part of the buildup
for the battle of Stalingrad, passed through that area. As a
consequence, the Germans made strenuous efforts to inter-
dict the traffic. They did this in part by surface raiders, but
mainly by massive submarine attacks. The allied response,
which was under Admiral Ingram's command, was carried
out by a number of old cruisers, a few destroyers, a large
number of sub-chasers, several squadrons of anti-submarine
airplanes, and a good part of the Brazilian Navy.

Admiral Ingram was a remarkable individual. A member
of the Annapolis class of 1907, where he was better known
for his athletic ability than for his intellectual performance,
Ingram had come up slowly and routinely in the peacetime
Navy. Heavyset, blunt in speech, he was thoroughly independent in word and deed. He was also one of the few Navy
officers who was not afraid of Admiral Ernest King, the cold

and aloof figure who was commander in chief of the United States Fleet and chief of naval operations. As is so often the case in such circumstances, Ingram's lack of fear of Admiral King made him one of the favorites of the commander in chief. On one occasion when Admiral Ingram was talking long distance in an office adjoining Admiral King's, the latter, hearing Ingram's booming voice, sent an aide to inquire whether Ingram was using the telephone or was trying to be heard direct and without electronic assistance. Very few other officers could have been the beneficiary of the great man's sense of humor.

Although thoroughly attentive to his duties in the South Atlantic, Ingram secretly wished that he could be assigned to some more active theater. His excess energies were expended in part in building comfortable accommodations for those under his command and in part by the procurement of luxurious accommodations for himself. The accommodations for the enlisted men included a base with elaborate recreational facilities in the port of Recife, as well as a comfortable rest and recreational center a few miles inland which was converted for that purpose from a partially completed Brazilian tuberculosis hospital. The accommodations for the admiral consisted principally of two yachts, which had been acquired by the Navy from their wealthy owners and assigned to Ingram. The yachts were moored side by side, so that the admiral could move from one to the other for his various meals and conferences at his whim. When dining with him, one could always be sure of a first-class meal, complete with wine and good Brazilian cigars.

The fact that the admiral served wine aboard his yachts arose out of an interesting encounter which took place somewhat earlier. On his way to attend his conference with Churchill and DeGaulle at Casablanca, President Roosevelt had paid a visit to Admiral Ingram at Belem, a port at the mouth of the Amazon River. The admiral had been advised that the president might ask for a drink and was accordingly well prepared. However, when the presidential request did in fact come, Ingram, tongue in cheek, reminded Roosevelt of the regulation forbidding alcoholic beverages aboard naval vessels. With a laugh, Roosevelt stated that the admiral should consider that he had a presidential dispensation, and with that the requested drinks were served. Whether the dispensation was meant to apply only for the occasion or for all time was not made clear. However, Ingram placed the latter interpretation upon it, at least during the period he was in the South Atlantic.

One of Ingram's most important functions in Brazil was more diplomatic than military. As the senior United States naval officer in the area, he had a good deal to say about the training of the small but growing Brazilian Navy, and also, by virtue of his close relationship with Admiral King, he had a significant influence upon the assignment of United States vessels and naval aircraft to the Brazilians under the Lend-Lease and other programs. The stories told elsewhere about the admiral's lighter side should not obscure the significant contribution which he made to the allied war effort in this and other regards. The fact that Brazil was one of the strongest and most dependable of our allies in South America was due in no small part, in my opinion, to Ingram's personal and diplomatic leadership.

Ingram was highly respected by the Brazilian government, including its president, Getulio Vargas. The high regard was due in some part to the naval materiel which he was able to deliver. But in large part it was due to his personality and to his method of operating. The American ambassador and the chiefs of a number of United States military missions were located in Rio de Janeiro. Ingram, however, steadfastly maintained his headquarters in the provincial city of Recife, a thousand miles from the capital. The consequence was that he remained aloof from the complications and intrigues surrounding the government, and his occasional descents upon the capital city were moments of undiluted triumph.

On one occasion Ingram took me with him to Rio. He had been invited by the president to sit in his box on September 7, the Brazilian national holiday, and to review the parade celebrating the event. When the admiral arrived at the president's box, the seats in the front row around the president were already largely occupied by functionaries of various degrees of importance. A lesser man than Ingram would have pushed his way through the group and gone directly to the president to make his presence known. Ingram's method, however, was different. He simply stood in the back of the box, his large figure looming over several rows of Brazilian and diplomatic personnel in front of him, until the president observed his arrival and came back to escort him personally to a seat which was made available in the front row.

On another occasion I was sent to Rio in the company of Lieutenant William T. Ingram, the admiral's son and flag lieutenant. Young Ingram was about my age and we were good friends. The purpose of this trip was for each of us to receive a decoration of the government of Brazil from the hands of Oswaldo Aranha, the distinguished and cultivated foreign minister. As Aranha pinned the Order of the Southern Cross on my uniform, he said, "I give you this decoration for three reasons. First, because you are a great-nephew of Elihu Root, who, second only to President Franklin D. Roosevelt, is known and respected in South America. Second, I give it to you because you are an attractive young man and I like you. Third, I give it to you because Admiral Ingram has told me to do so." Obviously, it was the third reason that mattered.

In June 1943 the allies landed in Sicily. After that it was possible for supplies to the Middle East and Asia to pass through the Mediterranean and the Suez Canal. The South Atlantic, which until then had been of great strategic significance, became a strategic backwash. For this reason and some others, I ardently hoped for a transfer to some more active theater. However, Ingram himself was of the same mind, and it was unlikely that he would be willing to help any of his close associates to be transferred until and unless he could arrange something for himself. I knew a number of people in Washington to whom I might have written for assistance, but all the mail from our headquarters was censored and this greatly inhibited any steps which I might have taken. Then there happened one of those extraordinary episodes which sometimes change a person's life.

The episode revolved around a visit to Admiral Ingram's headquarters by the secretary of the Navy, Frank Knox. When the secretary's plane landed at the airport outside the city, the admiral and all his senior officers went out to meet him, leaving me as virtually the only officer on the command floor of the headquarters building. I therefore deemed it my duty to stand at the elevator to greet the secretary upon his arrival at the building. As Secretary Knox emerged from the elevator, I stepped forward, shook his hand, and introduced myself. This being only three years after the very great notoriety I had received in the Willkie campaign, with which Knox, as a Republican member of the president's cabinet, was thoroughly familiar, he recognized my name. "What are you doing here?" he said. "You should be in some more active place." By this time Ingram had also emerged from the elevator and was standing alongside the secretary and me. The moment was ticklish and my heart was pumping madly. I wanted badly to be transferred, but clearly I could not afford to offend the admiral. "I am very happy here with Admiral Ingram," I replied. "However, sir, should you wish to order me to some more active theater, I would, of course, be honored to comply." The secretary said that he would see what could be done. Thereupon the group moved on and that was the last that I saw of him.

As the weeks following Secretary Knox's visit passed by and no orders came from Washington, my hopes sank. Obviously, the secretary had more important things to think about than the reassignment of a young Naval Reserve lieutenant. However, as I scratched my head and ruminated, I remembered a man named Adlai Stevenson whom I had met one evening the year before at dinner in Georgetown. In later years, of course, Adlai Stevenson served as governor of Illinois and was twice the candidate of the Democratic party for president, At this time, however, he was a civilian assistant to the secretary of the Navy. I took my courage in my hands and through the censorship I sent a letter to Stevenson in which, after reminding him of our meeting, I told him that when the secretary had passed through a number of weeks before, he had made an interesting comment. "If you have the opportunity," I wrote, "please ask your boss whether he really meant what he said." Apparently the secretary had meant it, because seventy-two hours later there came a dispatch ordering me to temporary duty in Washington and to ultimate assignment in Europe. One of the characteristics for which Adlai Stevenson was noted in later years was his loyalty to friends. Certainly he showed his generosity to me, a mere acquaintance.

That was not the end of the story, however. Since I had access to all dispatches received by the admiral, I knew of the arrival of the dispatch concerning me. But the action which had to be taken to effect the directive in the dispatch had to be taken by Ingram and his personnel officer, not by me. It was not long until I was summoned to the admiral's presence. "What is this?" he said, holding his copy of the dispatch in his hand. "Have you been dealing with someone behind my back in Washington?" "I cannot imagine how this came about," I replied innocently, "unless, sir, it has something to do with the remark that Secretary Knox made to me when he was here a number of weeks ago." "Well, it makes no difference," said the admiral, "because I will show you what I propose to do with it." Whereupon he crumpled the dispatch in his hand and threw it into the wastebasket. There being nothing left to say, I retired from his office to relate the story to Captain Braine, the chief of staff, who was my immediate superior.

Whether Captain Braine interceded for me or not, I never knew. However, a couple of days later I was again summoned to the admiral's presence. After asking me whether I really very much wanted to go, and being told that, much as I disliked leaving him, I would indeed appreciate the opportunity of going to a more active theater, the admiral invited me for dinner on his yacht and arranged transportation to Washington by air for the following day.

Later in the war, Admiral Ingram got his fourth star and became commander in chief of the Atlantic Fleet. In 1952 he died. I regret that I never saw him again after leaving his staff. Not only did I benefit much from his friendship and consideration, but he was a great example, especially in his relations with the Brazilians, of the effectiveness of a leader who relies more on instinct and personality than on intellect.

IV

It was on a dark day in December 1943 that I left New York for England as one of a number of naval officers who were passengers on the S.S. *Conestoga,* a brand-new tanker owned and operated by the Socony-Mobil Oil Company.

We travelled across the Atlantic in convoy, escorted by destroyers and an aircraft carrier. Because we took the southern route, the weather was comparatively warm and pleasant. It happened that one of the passengers was a Catholic chaplain, so that on Christmas Eve there was midnight mass on deck under the stars. Those among the crew who did not wish to attend mass took the duty of those who did, with the result that the attendance was large and impressive.

Upon arrival in London, I found that I had been assigned to the staff of Rear Admiral Alan G. Kirk, who had been designated to command the United States naval forces in the planned invasion of Normandy. Kirk was the finest type of naval officer. Of medium height, with clear blue eyes, at the age of fifty-six he was reaching the climax of a brilliant naval career. The year before he had commanded a task force under Vice Admiral Hewitt in the successful amphibious invasion of Sicily. In the performance of his military duties he was tough and authoritative, but relaxing on the tennis court or at the dinner table, both of which he enjoyed, he could be as civilized and sensitive and witty as one who had been trained to the arts. This combination of talents was of especial value to him later in life when, at the behest of Presidents Truman and Kennedy, he served at various times as our ambassador to Belgium, to the Soviet Union, and to the Republic of China.

The top commander of the allied invasion force was, of course, General Eisenhower. Under him were three British officers, in charge respectively of the combined armies, navies, and air forces. The officer in charge of the combined navies was Admiral Sir Bertram Ramsey. It was to him that Kirk, as Commander Western Task Force, reported.

The invasion was without doubt one of the great turning points of the war, and Kirk's role in it was generally and properly praised. On that day there were 2,400 vessels under his command, constituting the American part of the greatest armada ever assembled in the history of the world. So great was the success of that operation that one tends to forget some of the problems. It was not long after my arrival in London, however, that I began to learn about the problems and to learn further that some of them were not primarily military, but were problems of human pride and human rivalry.

Although it was fully understood that Kirk was to be in command of all United States forces in the invasion itself, there were complications and confusions in the planning stage and in the logistical buildup which should never have been permitted. One of the sources of these complications and confusions was the existence of a command called Commander United States Forces, Europe, which had been created long before the invasion was decided upon. The person holding that command was Admiral Harold Stark, who had been chief of naval operations at the time of Pearl Harbor and who wore four stars to Kirk's two. Kirk's personal relationship with Stark was excellent. Indeed, two years earlier he had served as Stark's chief of staff. But the lines of authority and responsibility of their respective commands were not always clear, and therein lay the trouble.

Thus, although Kirk had full operational responsibility and authority, he was required to deal with the fact of Stark's presence and seniority, especially in matters involving logistics and supplies, which were largely under the senior man's control. Whatever the intentions of the Navy Department in Washington may have been, the result was a diminution of the effective authority of the man upon whom the operational responsibility for the invasion rested. The failure to promote Kirk to vice admiral at that time added to the dimensions of the problem. It is true that his British counterpart was also a rear admiral, but his U.S. Army counterpart, Lieutenant General Bradley, had three stars to Kirk's two, and both of Kirk's immediate operational subordinates held rank equal to his own. Indeed, even his own chief of staff, Rear Admiral Struble, was his equal in rank. That he was able to maintain his authority and discharge his duties without the help to his prestige that a promotion would have given him was much to his credit. However, I never heard any complaint from Kirk himself on this subject. It was we members of his staff who were aware of the added difficulties this posed for him.

Unhappily, the rivalry in London was not limited to rivalry within the United States Navy. There was also rivalry between the Navy and the Army and, of course, between the Americans and the British. Indeed, as we observed some of the consequences of these rivalries, a number of my fellow junior officers and I used to express the hope that things were going even worse for the Germans on their side. The histories of the German effort which have been written since the war, based on documents which became available after the war, have established that this was in fact the case. Kirk's own relationship with the British was excellent, however, as can be drawn from the account of his first meeting with his British counterpart, Rear Admiral Sir Philip Vian. As they had a drink together, Kirk said to Vian, "I understand you have the reputation of being quite deaf and very rude," to which Vian replied, "I did not know I was deaf." From that moment on the two men were fast friends. Following the invasion, Kirk was invested as a Knight Commander of the Bath at the hands of King George VI.

Happily there were other aspects of the planning for the invasion which were more constructive. An outstanding example related to security. The date and the place for the invasion was set many months in advance. Taking into account all the staffs which were participating in the planning,

British and American, army, navy and air force, there must have been at least several hundred people who knew the crucial secret throughout the winter and spring of 1944. None of us had been the subject of the kind of exhaustive security checks which are routine today for persons having access to top-secret information. Nevertheless, not only were the Germans surprised by the attack, as history has established, but even the American newspapermen assigned to the armed forces were uninformed until the official briefings immediately prior to the invasion itself. I was present at the pre-departure briefing given to the press by Admiral Kirk, and I will never forget the suspense in the room as he raised his pointer to the spot on the map where the troops were to land.

In May Kirk and his staff moved from London to Plymouth, awaiting the arrival of the heavy cruiser *Augusta,* which was to be his flagship. The *Augusta* had already achieved its place in history as the setting for the signing in 1943 by Roosevelt and Churchill of the Atlantic Charter. It was now to play its second crucial role.

One of my close friends on the staff was Roger L. Putnam, the former mayor of Springfield, Massachusetts. Roger had served as a very young man in World War I, and, as a result of his friendship with Kirk, had succeeded in getting himself again commissioned at an age considerably more advanced than was usually acceptable. His friendship with Kirk also resulted in his having a special luxury in which I and others of his friends shared.

Before leaving the United States for London, Roger donated to the Navy a convertible Buick sedan which he had used as mayor of Springfield and which was appropriately fitted out with an official siren. The car was assigned by the Navy Department as part of Kirk's pool in England, and Roger was able to use it, not only in connection with his official duties, but occasionally also on outings which were perhaps slightly less than official. As we drove along the roads of the beautiful Devon countryside, we stopped from time to time to give a lift to some hitchhiking servicemen. On such occasions, Roger frequently gave himself and his passengers the thrill of unexpectedly opening up the official siren.

So much has been written about the invasion of Normandy that it would serve no useful purpose for me here to try to give historical or military details. I will limit myself, therefore, to a few personal footnotes, which the reader may find interesting or amusing.

To have participated in that great event in any capacity was a tremendous experience. It was a beautiful evening on June 5 as our section of the vast armada set sail from Plymouth. By that time it was no secret that momentous events were underway. Thousands of English people, waving their handkerchiefs in the twilight, lined the shore as we moved out of the harbor. Standing on the deck surveying the scene, we on shipboard knew that the next morning and in the days following the future of civilization would be determined, for good or ill.

The military and naval operation was complex and intricate. Officers more senior and experienced than I stood watches on the flag bridge, representing the admiral. Because of my junior rank and lack of naval training, my duties were mostly below decks, and they related more to logistics than to operations. One of the unexpected dividends of my position on so exalted a staff, however, was an opportunity which came to me one day, about ten days after the landings, to repay a debt to a close friend of my childhood.

When I was a boy, my family used to spend the summers on eastern Long Island. One of my good friends in those adolescent and pre-adolescent years was Charles S. Potter, now a senior officer in the company which owns the International Amphitheater and the Stockyards Inn in Chicago. Ours was a close and relaxed relationship, but in one respect it was out of balance. My family was a great deal stricter than his, with the consequence that he rather than I generally supplied the means and milieu of our joint activities. To put it another way, I was the beneficiary of our fun together, and he was the provider.

The Potters owned the sailboat in which we sailed, and it was Charlie who taught me to sail. The Potters allowed their children to use the family car whereas mine did not, and so it was Charlie who taught me to drive. The Potters arranged for their boys to go with friends on camping trips to Montauk Point, then a true wilderness country, and it was Charlie and his brothers who taught me how to sleep and cook and take care of myself in the outdoors. I cannot say I felt any guilt at that young age for being so clearly on the long end of the bargain of our friendship, but I did often wish that the give and take might be more equal. Certainly, the thought that I might some day be able to turn the tables and repay the debt never occurred to me then. But the opportunity to do so did come, quite unexpectedly, in the following manner.

Having responded to a summons to Admiral Kirk's cabin, I was told that I was to deliver an important confidential message into the personal hands of a senior U.S. Army officer then located on Utah Beach, about thirty miles across the Bay of the Seine from Omaha Beach, off which the *Augusta* lay at anchor. My means of transportation was to be a PT boat, several of which had been detached from direct military activities to serve as special transport for communications missions of high priority.

As we sped across the Bay of the Seine, I recalled that my old friend Charlie Potter was in command of the Second

Beach Battalion, which had been part of the initial landings on Utah Beach ten days previously. Since a beach battalion's duties relate primarily to the early stages of an amphibious landing, I assumed that he was probably no longer there. And I realized that even if he were there, the chances of finding him in that large and active area were remote, to say the least. Nevertheless, I determined to try.

By extraordinary good luck I did find him through the good offices of the senior Army officer to whom my mission from Admiral Kirk had directed me. As it happened, I found him at the moment that he and a group of his fellow officers were about to eat their C rations around a small fire they had built at the rear of the beach. They invited me to join them.

It was hardly a luxurious meal. Although most of the Germans had by this time been driven back from the coastal areas, there were still a few pockets of enemy resistance near the beach, and as we ate, an occasional shell burst in the vicinity. On top of that, it was raining and it was cold.

I tried to lighten the conversation as we ate by reminiscing about the days long ago when we cooked and ate together on the moors and beaches of Montauk. But in my heart I felt a terrible guilt, founded in the knowledge that when we finished I would return via my multimillion-dollar ferry to the warm showers and dry sheets of the *Augusta*, leaving Charlie to spend this night and succeeding nights in the wet and the cold. My feelings were intensified when he told me that the function of the Second Beach Battalion had long since been completed, that by then it should have been evacuated, but that in the press and confusion of the events of those days it had apparently been forgotten.

Having finished our spare meal, I took my leave, returned to the flagship and made my way to Admiral Kirk's cabin. After reporting the successful completion of the mission to which he had assigned me, I turned to go. As I did so, the admiral said, "Oren, did you observe anything else that I should know about?" "Nothing, sir," I replied, "except perhaps that the Second Beach Battalion is still on the beach." Then came the words that repaid my childhood debt of long ago. "There's no need for the beach battalion to be on the beach at this stage," said the admiral. "Draft a dispatch ordering them back to England at once." He waited while I wrote the order and then he initialed it. I personally delivered the precious document to the flag communications officer. The next night Charlie Potter and his fellow officers and men slept in dry beds in Plymouth.

As the allied armies pushed inland, the situation off the beaches became less tense. Indeed, there came a time when it had calmed down to the point where less experienced officers, such as myself, were allowed to stand watch on the flag bridge. The admiral and the chief of staff were never more than minutes away, so at that relatively late period in the invasion the risk resulting from my lack of naval training was small. My first duty of this sort was the midwatch, which ran from midnight until four in the morning. As I stood my watch I noticed a fire developing on the beach some miles away, but did not think it of any great consequence. After a while the ship's duty officer, representing the captain of the ship, came to the flag bridge to ask whether I had reported the fire to the admiral, to which I replied that I had not. Somewhat later, the same officer returned to say that the captain was of the opinion that the admiral should be advised of the existence of the fire. In the light of my inexperience and the fact that this was my first watch on the bridge, I concluded that two hints were enough. Accordingly, since I still did not want to disturb the admiral myself, I sent word requesting that Admiral Struble, the chief of staff, come to the bridge. By the time Admiral Struble appeared a few minutes later, the fire had subsided to such a degree that he had difficulty finding it. In an effort to help him I said, "Over there, sir, off the port bow," and went on to apologize for disturbing him, explaining that I had done so only at the insistence of the captain. Admiral Struble finally saw the fire, which by this time was virtually extinguished. He nevertheless thanked me for calling him and said I had done the right thing. As he turned to leave the bridge, he said, "By the way, Root, that is the starboard quarter, not the port bow." It *was* dark and we *were* at anchor. However, it will thus be understood why it was not until two weeks after the invasion that officers of my experience were assigned to watch on the bridge.

A number of weeks after the landings, the *Augusta* was sent to the Mediterranean in preparation for the assault upon the south of France which took place in mid-August of that year. Accordingly, Admiral Kirk transferred his flag to the *Thompson*, a destroyer. The *Thompson* had room for only ten of the admiral's staff of sixty, and I was much pleased and complimented when I was invited to be one of the ten.

On June 29 Cherbourg, the great French port at the tip of the Cotentin Peninsula, fell to the American armies. Kirk wished to inspect the port and invited members of his staff to accompany him. It was necessary, however, for one member of the staff to remain behind to stand the flag watch. Since everybody wanted to go, lots were drawn to determine who should stay behind, and I lost the draw. Thus it was that I, who, as a staff officer, had at no time during my four and one-half years of active duty had a single person under my direct military command, was, for the two hours that the admiral was ashore, the acting commander of a fleet comprising many thousands of men.

Shortly thereafter, the admiral returned to London and

most of his staff were dispersed. The promotion which was withheld from him when he most needed it came in September of that year, with still another upon his retirement in 1946. Although my service with him came to an end after Normandy, our friendship continued until his death in 1963. Both in the remaining part of his wartime duties and in his later diplomatic assignments, he made significant contributions to the welfare of his country.

V

I hope that the accounts in this chapter of some of the lighter sides of my war experiences do not lead anybody to believe that I was insensitive to the war's tragedies and sufferings. Nobody who lived through that period, and certainly nobody who served in the armed forces, could be unaware of the millions of battle casualties on both sides and the millions of civilians, including women and children, who were killed or bombed out of their homes and livelihoods in what were, until Vietnam, the most savage bombardments of history. Nor can one or should one deny or forget the cruelties and the degradation of the human spirit which accompanied many aspects of that awful conflict. Among the military there was also frequent boredom, and the loneliness which comes from long enforced separation from home and family.

But in the perversity of human nature, the war had its glories as well as its tragedies. There was the valor of the R.A.F. in the Battle of Britain, of the volunteers at Dunkirk, of the defenders of Stalingrad, of the French Resistance and of course of the troops who stormed the beaches of Normandy and the islands of the Pacific. As is so often the case with human nature, along with the cruelties and the degredation engendered by the war, the sufferings and the demands for sacrifice brought out the best in people. In our own country and among our own fighting men, while there were few of the martial bands and sentimental songs of World War I, there was a real sense of purpose and a conviction that, with all its horrors and miseries, the war could be the prelude to a saner and better world.

In October 1944, after my return from Normandy, I was invited by Mrs. Ogden Reid to address the *Herald Tribune* Forum in the Grand Ballroom of the Waldorf-Astoria Hotel and over a nationwide radio network. There were other speakers who spoke from other points of view. My assignment was to say something on behalf of those fighting in the Atlantic and in Europe. On that occasion I spoke as follows:

There are hundreds of young naval officers who have a better right than I have to be speaking to you for the Navy tonight. I am here partly by accident and partly because as a member of Rear Admiral Kirk's staff I did participate in the invasion of Normandy and in the many months of detailed planning which preceded it.

I want to give you two quick impressions of the young Americans who took part in that invasion. What I have to say applies to both the Army and the Navy, because ours was an amphibious assault and we acted as a team.

In the first place, you realize that most of the young Americans who landed in Normandy on June 6 and thereafter had been in Britain for many months before that—waiting and training and then waiting some more. Some were swarming ashore from Navy ships in Britain's overcrowded ports, others living and working in hundreds of Britain's tiny war-rationed villages. It was not an easy situation either for the British or for us. Yet it worked without a single serious hitch. It worked partly because of the magnificent understanding of the British people.

But it it worked, too, because of the conduct of our own men. Whether they were sweating it out in maneuvers and practice landings, whether they were relaxing in the evenings at pubs or with British girls, whether they were trooping to church on Sundays in numbers which many observers could scarcely believe, these men were a credit to America. Just to see them and to be one of them made one proud to be an American.

The other impression is of the same men on D-Day and thereafter. Because he believed that one of the great advantages Americans have over some other people lies in their ability to be self-reliant and to improvise, Admiral Kirk insisted that every officer and man of his task force be informed of the general overall naval plan prior to landing. The result was that when details of the operation could not be carried out exactly as planned—and no operation is ever perfect—these officers and men were in a position to improvise methods by which the broad objective could be achieved. And they did just that. To the fact that they did is owed in large measure the success of the assault. To see a young lieutenant, or a young boatswain's mate take hold of a messy situation in his particular area and straighten it out on his own initiative was for anybody who saw it an inspiring and heart-lifting experience. That, too, made one proud to be an American.

I do not mean to suggest that the men who participated in the Normandy landings were any better than the men who have fought and are fighting our battles in other areas of the world. Nor do I mean to say that they were supermen. Actually, they were just average young Americans, no more and no less. But from what I saw, I will stake my life upon the proposition that neither in the world today nor in all history has there been a finer aggregation of men than those who today comprise the armed forces of the United States.

If anybody can build a decent world ahead, these men will do it. Given adequate leadership when they return, given a fair opportunity to appraise the facts and given a challenge to their better selves, these men will never let us down.

There were a good many Americans, including a significant percentage of the armed forces, who were determined to do what they could to contribute to the post-war leadership to which I referred in my talk. By strange coincidence, two of us who were so determined were sitting, unknown to each other, on the same platform on the same night at the *Herald Tribune* Forum.

CHAPTER THREE

The American Veterans Committee

I

It is unusual for a veterans organization to be conceived even before the beginning of the war from which the veterans are to come. But that was what happened in the case of the American Veterans Committee. Little did those of us who conceived that organization know that in the immediate post-war years it would play a small but significant role in the then-important Cold War struggle between the United States and the Soviet Union. The story of how AVC came into being and of the role it played in the Cold War is a dramatic story and it is worth telling.

In the summer of 1941, when I was on active duty in the Navy Supply Office at 90 Church Street in New York City,

I received a telephone call from Gilbert A. Harrison, who said he would like to come to see me to discuss post-war political matters. That was several months before the attack on Pearl Harbor brought us into the war.

Gilbert Harrison, who is presently the editor-in-chief of *The New Republic,* was at that time a young man in his twenties, employed in the Office of Civilian Defense in Washington. He had no doubt that the United States would be in the war before long and believed that it was none too soon to begin discussing the kind of society which would follow the war, and specifically the kind of veterans group which would be organized when that time came.

In the period between World War I and World War II, the veterans organizations had been among the country's most powerful political influences. The American Legion and the Veterans of Foreign Wars, in particular, were forces to be reckoned with, both at the local level, where the individual posts functioned, and at the national level. Primarily as a result of their efforts, bonus bills involving substantial financial payments to veterans were passed by the Congress over the vetoes of two presidents, including President Roosevelt's at a time when he was at the height of his political power and prestige. At the local level, veterans' posts had usually been pleasant centers for drinking beer and for social comradeship. If they had any ideological orientation, it was generally conservative and in support of the largely self-centered and nationalistic objectives of their national organization.

Gil Harrison and I met often during the summer of 1941, usually in my mother's apartment in New York City, where I then lived. We agreed that the veterans organization which would follow World War II should be very different from the earlier ones, that its object should be to benefit society as a whole, rather than primarily its own members.

Even though the United States was not yet in the war, we knew how we would feel when we were in it. We would feel that war was a terrible price for any society to pay, and that for the price to have been worth paying there should be a constructive result, even beyond victory. In other words, we were young idealists, determined that out of all the suffering and holocausts we saw ahead there should emerge at the end at least one organization committed to the objective of making that suffering and those holocausts worthwhile. In the course of our discussions, therefore, we began the outlines of a set of principles which might form the basis for a new group to be formed when the war was over. We never got to the point, however, of giving it a name.

Following that summer, Gil Harrison's and my paths diverged. He joined the Army and I was transferred first to Washington and then overseas. I was generally aware of the fact that the discussions he and I had had were being carried forward in correspondence among a number of servicemen, but I took no part in that correspondence, and it was not until later that I learned about it in some detail.

On the night of October 16, 1944, I made the talk at the *Herald Tribune* Forum referred to in the last chapter. Later in the same program Charles G. Bolte, a young American who had served with the British Army and had lost a leg at the battle of El Alamein, was introduced. In the course of his speech, he described a new veterans organization, the American Veterans Committee, which was in the process of formation. As he read the "statement of intentions" which constituted the basic principles of that organization, I heard coming from his lips some of the ideas and, in a few cases, some of the very words which Gil Harrison and I had worked on over three years earlier in my mother's apartment. Could this new organization be the product of those discussions? The "statement of intentions" of the AVC as read by Charles Bolte to the audience in the Grand Ballroom of the Waldorf-Astoria that evening was as follows:

We look forward to being civilians: making a decent living, raising a family, and living in freedom from the threat of another war. But that was what most Americans wanted from the last war. They found that military victory does not automatically bring peace, jobs, or freedom. To guarantee our interests, which are those of our country, we must work for what we want.

Therefore, we are associating ourselves with American men and women regardless of race, creed, or color, who are serving with or have been honorably discharged from our armed forces, merchant marine, or allied forces. When we are demobilized it will be up to all of us to decide what action can best further our aims.

These will include: Aid for every veteran and his family during demobilization. A job for every veteran, with private enterprise and government working together to provide full employment for the nation. Thorough social security. Free speech, press, worship, assembly, and ballot. Disarmament of Germany and Japan and the elimination of the power of their militarist classes. Continuance of the United Nations as partners, acting together to stop any threat to peace.

I could hardly wait for the program to come to an end. As soon as it did, I went up to Bolte and found, as I had suspected, that the AVC had indeed developed from Gil Harrison's initiative and that he, Bolte, was its current executive head. We thereupon repaired, with his attractive wife Mary, across the street to a *boîte* called the Glass Hat, where we talked into the morning. I learned that in the years since I had seen Gil Harrison the ideas he and I had discussed in the summer of 1941 had been expanded and developed through a "committee of correspondents," composed of men in various parts of the military service all over the world. By early 1944 the process had developed to the point that the organization needed executive leadership and Bolte, who was available, undertook to provide it. He considered himself a kind of trustee of the organization until the war was over and until its structure could be formalized by the veterans who would by that time have returned. The title "Committee" was chosen to emphasize its temporary status.

II

There was, of course, no assurance that World War II veterans would want a new organization or, even if they did, that that organization would be the AVC. The established groups—the American Legion, the Veterans of Foreign Wars, and others—made great efforts to attract the new veterans to their membership, and many joined up. However, there were a significant number of people coming out of World War II who believed that they should have their own organization and that it should be different from those of the past. Idealism ran high in those days and there were many veterans, especially those with propensities for leadership, who were not willing to settle for the kind of largely self-centered organization which had dominated the period between World War I and World War II.

AVC was not the only new veterans group to be organized, of course, but more than most others it attracted a number of persons with prominent names. Partly for that reason, and partly because of the colorful and articulate leadership provided by Bolte and Harrison and the people they gathered around them, AVC acquired an influence out of proportion to its numbers. Among the persons who were associated with it in positions of leadership in those early years were Franklin D. Roosevelt, Jr., the son of the late president; Robert R. Nathan, an economist who had held important government posts and was close to the top labor leadership of the country; Cord Meyer, Jr., the head of United World Federalists and later the holder of an important appointment in the Central Intelligence Agency; Richard Bolling, who soon became and still is a distinguished member of the House of Representatives; Hubert Will, who is today a judge of the United States District Court in Illinois; Merle Miller, the author; Michael Straight, who was then publisher of *The New Republic*, whose father, Willard Straight, had served with distinction in World War I; and many others.

AVC, together with the older veterans groups, was concerned with matters of interest primarily to veterans, such as the proper functioning of the Veterans Administration and the availability of needed medical assistance. But it differed significantly from other veterans groups in emphasizing the welfare of the whole community and the world as well. Its motto called for "a more democratic and prosperous America in a more stable world." It took this position not because of lack of interest in the veteran, but out of the conviction that in the last analysis the veteran could benefit only as a member of an improved society.

Thus in the domestic arena, AVC argued that the conferring of particular rights on veterans with respect to jobs would not of itself provide jobs for veterans. Only if there were jobs for all would the veteran's job be assured. Full employment became AVC's objective, because it believed that without full employment the special benefits for the veteran could lead in the end to the breadline.

In the international arena, AVC stood foursquare for international cooperation to keep the peace. Young as the organization was, it was invited by the State Department, together with some of the older veterans groups, to send representatives to San Francisco to act as consultants to the United Nations Conference in 1945. Somewhat later, AVC became a strong supporter of the Marshall Plan and of the North Atlantic Alliance, unlike other veterans groups, which were more equivocal on these subjects.

III

In human affairs events rarely turn out as they are planned, and in that truism there lay ahead much drama for AVC. The founders and early members of AVC hoped and expected that its principal accomplishment would be to bring a liberal and public-spirited force to bear upon the country's post-war policies, both domestic and international. As the year 1946 unfolded, however, it became increasingly apparent that AVC's major activity, at least in its early period, would be to play a small but significant role in the Cold War between the Soviet Union and the United States.

In order to understand the situation, it is necessary to recall that in those early post-war years the policy of the Soviet Union included the support in other countries of groups and organizations sympathetic to its interests, with a view to influencing the policies of those countries and, hopefully, of gaining control in the long run of their governments. Thus, in France, Italy, the United Kingdom, and other countries of western Europe, groups sympathetic to and financed at least in part by the Soviet Union achieved important representation in the labor movements of those countries and, in some cases, significant representation in their parliaments. In the 1948 elections in Italy, a major effort was made by the Communist party and its political allies to take over the government. That this effort failed was due in no small part to the Marshall Plan and to an extraordinary barrage of anti-communist letters from persons of Italian descent in the United States addressed to families and friends in Italy.

The philosophy of these Soviet-oriented groups was socialist, but it differed from old-line socialism in that its true objective was not reform but the creation of chaos and disorder, with a view to the ultimate seizure of power by persons responsive to the interests of the Soviet Union. In the United States the principal instrumentality for such groups was the American Communist party, and their principal organ was the *Daily Worker*. The strategy of the party was to infiltrate and ultimately to take over existing organizations with significant present or potential influence in the community. Thus, at various times major assaults were made on the great labor unions, especially those with socialist or quasi-socialist orientation. Though similar efforts to infiltrate the labor movements in the countries of western Europe were to a large degree successful, in the United States they were uniformly deflected. This deflection was accomplished under the leadership of a number of individual giants, including Philip Murray of the Steel Workers, Walter Reuther of the Automobile Workers, David Dubinsky and Jacob Potofsky of the clothing unions, and others. The fact that the labor movement in the United States, uniquely in the western world, rejected the communist threat is due to the courage, intelligence, and patriotism of these great men to whom their countrymen owe, on that account, a very great debt of gratitude.

Prior to 1946 there was evidence that the Communist party in the United States was seeking a foothold in the American Legion. Because of the size of the Legion as well as its tightly organized leadership, however, they were not making much progress. The American Veterans Committee, being very small, new, loosely organized, and led by a group of relatively inexperienced idealists, seemed a better target.

Accordingly, sometime in late 1945 or early 1946, the policy of the Communist party shifted, and its target among veterans groups ceased to be the American Legion and became, instead, the AVC.

During the winter of 1946, the National Planning Committee, the top governing body of AVC of which I was a member, met regularly. Its functions were to develop the organization's membership, which was growing rapidly, and to prepare for the first national convention, which was scheduled to be held in Des Moines, Iowa, in June of that year, at which convention the formal structure and policy of the organization would be established. As the winter progressed, it became increasingly apparent to a number of us in the AVC leadership that there were people within the organization who were viewing the issues presented not so much from the point of view of the welfare of AVC or of the United States, but from the point of view of the Communist party and of the Soviet Union.

That people sympathetic to the views of the Communist party were seeking to influence and probably dominate AVC was ackowledged more readily by some of the top leaders of the organization than by others. Inasmuch as all of the leaders were idealists and for the most part held political philosophies somewhat to the left of center, they were reluctant to become known as "red baiters." As a strong believer in free speech and individual liberty myself, I was no more anxious than anybody else to be so tainted. On the other hand, neither did I want to see the organization taken over by persons whose primary interests lay outside our country, nor did I wish to be personally associated with any such debacle. I felt I needed help. As it turned out, the person to whom I went was the best of all people to provide such help. That person was David Dubinsky, president of the International Ladies Garment Workers Union.

89

David Dubinsky was an old-line socialist who had emigrated to the United States from his native Russia at the age of nineteen. As an early member of the trade union movement, he participated in the struggle for economic and social recognition for the workers, and that path led him ultimately to the presidency of his union. When the Communist party and its sympathizers sought to infiltrate and dominate the union, he led the fight against them and threw them out. Somewhat later, he faced a similar threat within the American Labor party, a small labor-oriented third party which played a major role in the election of Fiorello La Guardia as mayor of New York City. When the communists moved to take control of that party, the noncommunist leadership broke away to form the Liberal party. The principal leaders of that breakaway were Alex Rose, president of the Hatters Union, and David Dubinsky. A man of small physical stature but great intellectual and personal power, David Dubinsky was probably one of the most experienced fighters against communism in the United States. Clearly I had gone to the right man.

It was early in the winter of 1946 that I spent an hour with Dubinsky in his office. I told him what I thought was happening in AVC and asked his advice about how to deal with it. In the course of our conversation we also briefly discussed the Republican party, and I expressed the hope that the party would not forget the legacy of Wendell Willkie and would develop along liberal lines.

Dubinsky heard me out with courtesy, and he expressed sympathy for the predicament in which my colleagues and I found ourselves, but in the end he was not encouraging. "A bunch of silk-stocking idealists such as you," he said, "have about as much chance of beating the Communist party in AVC as you have of liberalizing the Republican party." He patted me paternally on the back, and I left, reinforced in my view that the communist threat must be met, but still uncertain as to how to proceed.

As it turned out, my visit to Dubinsky was more effective than I could have dared to hope. Shortly after the meeting, two men named Gus Tyler and Murray Gross appeared before the National Planning Committee to apply for a charter for a new chapter in New York City. Otherwise unidentified on that occasion, it was later learned that Tyler and Gross were members of the International Ladies Garment Workers Union and that Dubinsky had stimulated their interest in making the application for a charter. The charter was granted and it was not long thereafter that Gus Tyler became one of the principal strategists and tacticians in the fight against communist influence in AVC, bringing to bear not only his native intelligence and energies, but also the vast experience and, to some extent, the resources of his union. Murray Gross played an important but lesser role in the early stages of the struggle, and in later years he was elected national chairman of AVC. In the light of the major contribution made by these men, and particularly by Tyler, it can perhaps be said that my visit to Dubinsky was decisive in the life of AVC.

As the winter progressed, it became clear that the question of whether AVC would be dominated by communist sympathizers or by noncommunist liberals would be determined by the convention in Des Moines. That convention would be called upon to select seventeen members of a new National Planning Committee, as well as the top national officers. By the time the convention met, the candidacy of Charles Bolte, who was standing for reelection as the noncommunist national chairman, was so strong that the communist sympathizers decided not to challenge it. They decided instead to make the issue at other levels.

One of the tactics of the Communist party and its sympathizers in those days, which had frequently been successful in other groups, was simply to outlast their opposition. Many members of good will of other organizations, having regular jobs and obligations outside those organizations, reached a point in the course of lengthy discussions at meetings that they simply could not stay any longer and went home, leaving the field to the communists. As part of their tactics, the communists also resorted to every possible procedural delay, trying to exhaust their opponents and cause them to leave. At Des Moines, however, none of these tactics was successful. The noncommunist leadership of AVC, which controlled the temporary machinery of the convention, had mastered the procedural techniques to an extent which made them fully the equals of their opponents in this respect. The great moment came during the third night of the convention, after the noncommunist group had won a series of critical votes. At this point, contrary to the experience in many other organizations which had gone down before the communist threat, it was the communist sympathizers who went home, leaving the noncommunist leadership in the hall, sleepy and bedraggled, but successful.

One of the best summaries of the convention was made by Thomas L. Stokes, the well-known Scripps-Howard columnist, who wrote as follows from Des Moines under the date of June 17, 1946:

> An inspiring miracle is perhaps a good description of the performance of the 850 World War II veteran delegates who, working day and night, created the permanent organization of the American Veterans Committee at the first annual convention here and charted a progressive course on domestic and foreign policy.
>
> These earnest youngsters will be heard from, and so will the others they enlist as they go home to expand from their present 80,000 membership and exert their influence on affairs of their communities, the nation and the world.

This convention was something such as was never seen before by this writer in 25 years of covering national and state political and other conventions. It was a fine antidote for the cynicism beginning to spread again through America and the world.

The youngsters had to go through the same mechanics of all political conventions. They worked all night long in delegation caucuses, and in platform constitution and nominating sessions. They had to learn as they went along. There were no high jinks, no drunkenness or disorderliness, no dropping of paper bags of water from 11th-story hotel windows, no parades—nothing but business.

They had no time or inclination for anything else. They got their job done by sticking to it for four days, though sometimes it looked as if they wouldn't. Altogether, they were a group of ruggedly individualistic, independent, thinking young men and women and deadly in earnest that this worst of all wars shall not have been fought in vain.

But there were some few professionals here, a tiny minority with Communist leanings, come here to confuse, to work their way in. They worked at it ceaselessly. They had the advantage of experience. Their strategy was obvious.

It is to the credit of the leadership, including Charles G. Bolte, national chairman; Gilbert Harrison of Los Angeles, one of the founders; Franklin D. Roosevelt, Jr., Oren Root, Jr., and some others, that they decided to meet this issue head-on, without compromise, and quash it. They did. All liberal organizations these days have this problem. This one, unlike some of the others, decided to face it squarely.

The battle at the Des Moines convention was a major victory, but it did not win the war and those sympathetic to the communist cause continued to fight. The national leadership, by this time thoroughly aware that the magnitude of the stakes overcame any risk of being called "red baiters," fought back. In November 1946 the National Planning Committee adopted a Statement on Communism. After rehearsing something of the history and purposes of AVC, the statement alluded to the record of infiltration and destruction of other liberal groups by the American Communist party and its sympathizers and concluded with the following words: "the Communist Party rejects the basic convictions of the true American progressive. AVC as an organization of veterans loyal to the tradition of individual liberty can follow no other course than one of conscientious objection to the unprogressive, totalitarian doctrines of the American Communist Party. Those whom we ask to join AVC have a right to know the principles underlying this organization and its leadership. We oppose the entrance into our ranks of members of the Communist Party and we shall strive to prevent them, when and if, by subterfuge or deceit, they gain such entrance, from attempting to use AVC as a sounding-board for their own perverse philosophy." Although there was no threat to AVC from the right, it was deemed wise to balance the above statement with a Statement on Fascism. Both statements were submitted to all chapters for approval or disapproval, with the resulting vote being preponderantly but not overwhelmingly for approval.

The second annual AVC convention took place in Milwaukee the following spring. The issues and the personalities were very much the same as they had been in Des Moines the year before. This time, however, the noncommunist forces achieved even larger majorities. The third and fourth annual conventions in Cleveland and Chicago, respectively, resulted in total victory against the communist sympathizers, after which they ceased to be a significant influence in the organization.

In the years which followed, AVC continued to function and remains to this day an effective force for constructive goals. However, the tremendous internal struggle cost so much in time, energy, and money that the early momentum of the organization was lost. The high point of membership was probably about one hundred thousand, and that was probably sometime between the first and second conventions.

It would be futile to guess the path which AVC might have followed had the communist assault not transpired. Suffice it to say that it met that assault head-on and by so doing made a perhaps small but indubitably significant contribution to the preservation of independence and freedom in our society. Indeed, had the struggles of the Cold War been less successful, the current era of rapprochement with the Soviet Union might never have taken place.

An incidentally constructive consequence of AVC's early struggles can be found in the number of persons involved in those struggles who went on to national prominence and public office. These included Orville Freeman, who became governor of Minnesota and secretary of agriculture; G. Mennen Williams, who was four times elected governor of Michigan, and held many other high government posts; Hubert R. Will, presently a judge of the United States District Court in Illinois; Jacob K. Javits, successively a member of the House of Representatives and United States Senator from New York; and many others.

IV

Viewed from the place in time from which this book is written, the question may fairly be asked to what extent the generation which came back from World War II fulfilled its dreams. We had high aspirations and we were often critical of those who had gone before us. How then did we come out?

The answer, I believe, is a two-sided one. Clearly we did not fulfill *all* our dreams. But both in domestic and in foreign affairs we have made significant progress. If we have not solved our problems, at least we have dealt with them in a reasonably constructive way.

Or maybe the point would be better made were I to say that while the generation which came out of World War II definitely did not fulfill all its dreams, it has at least given birth to a new generation which is determined to do so. And this is something of which, with all our current problems, the World War II generation can definitely be proud. In the usual course of events, idealism gives way to cynicism and vice versa. So the hope and idealism of those of us who came out of World War II could very well have turned into frustration and selfishness in the next generation Instead of that, the younger generation today—at least that part of it which is most vocal—holds against us not our idealism but our failure to live up to that idealism. They are determined to fulfill our ancient dreams. This may in the end be our greatest accomplishment.

But what else did we accomplish in the twenty-eight years since World War II came to an end? What is the balance sheet for that period, for us in the United States and for the world and for mankind?

Certainly in material matters there have been great advances. Gross national product, per capita income, savings and investment, all these have multiplied manyfold. While poverty continues to exist in undesirable quantities, it has nevertheless been reduced to a percentage level lower than ever before in history.

But there have been other tremendous changes, too. One of the great issues of 1948 was whether there should be a Federal Fair Employment Practice Act—a principle which today is wholly accepted. In the period since World War II, we have had the landmark decision of the Supreme Court of the United States in *Brown* vs. *Board of Education,* which established the standard of equality in education, and we have had a President of the United States from the southern state of Texas who wholeheartedly embraced that decision. Clearly neither the courts nor the chief executive has solved our problems of racial inequity. But we have come a long way since President Franklin Roosevelt had to issue a special order to bring about integration of the government cafeterias in wartime Washington, something we now take wholly for granted.

In the years since World War II, there have been vast changes in the areas of religion and of sex, in the role of educational institutions and of families, and in dozens of other aspects of our lives. Some of the changes have been clearly for the good, some more arguable, but we have adapted to them all, and we are reasonably poised to deal with those which lie ahead.

In international matters, the record is at least as impressive as it is in domestic matters. The western world is still a free society, and this is due in large part to such American initiatives as the Marshall Plan and President Truman's great decisions in Greece, Turkey, and Korea. It is due, too, to a fact which history cannot overlook, which is that for nearly a generation following Hiroshima and Nagasaki, the United States had a nuclear monopoly of which it did not take advantage. And now in the SALT talks, not only those which have transpired but those which hopefully lie ahead, we are prepared to share the advantages and mute the terrors of the nuclear capacities of our society and that of the Soviet Union. Indeed we were prepared to do so as early as 1946, when Bernard Baruch put forward his proposals for limitation of nuclear armament based on mutual inspection. The rejection of that plan by the Soviet Union may in retrospect be regarded as one of the major tragedies of history.

In striking the balance sheet of our generation, one cannot, of course, overlook Vietnam, which was probably the most complex and divisive issue of those times. From one point of view, it was the most immoral and unnecessary act of our national life. From the other point of view, it was an unavoidable sacrifice in the maintenance of stability and long-term peace in our unstable and atavistic world. Maybe our descendants will know the answer a hundred years from now. An accomplishment upon which all will agree, however, is the growing rapprochement between the United States on the one hand and the Soviet Union and the People's Republic of China on the other, thus beginning a reversal of a long and unhappy period of misunderstanding.

Another fact which should be remembered is that the generation which came out of World War II is responsible for much, but not for everything. That generation itself inherited a world which it did not make and genes which it did not create. Given this world, and given those genes, the accomplishments of the generation since the allied victory in Europe and Asia in 1945 have been a great deal more good than bad.

Let us also remember that the first responsibility of any society is to survive, and that we have done. In the years since the end of World War II our society has survived, not only physically and materially, but politically and spiritually. We have not been perfect. We have made mistakes, some of them pretty big ones. But we have survived. Let us hope that our free society will survive our children's generation as well as it has survived our own. And let us hope, in addition, that our children will indeed perfect our dreams.

CHAPTER FOUR

Post-War Politics in New York State— The Early Years

I

In New York State the era since World War II has been dominated by two men, Thomas E. Dewey and Nelson A. Rockefeller. With the exception of the four years during which Averell Harriman was governor, these two men have occupied the Executive Mansion from 1943 to the present time. It has been my good fortune to know them both, and, in the case of Rockefeller, to work for him for five years. In order to see these public figures in perspective, however, as well as to understand other public men, such as Jacob K.

Javits and John V. Lindsay, who also played significant roles in the same period, it is necessary first to review some aspects of the history of the Republican party, and to recapture the political situation as it was in the country and in New York State when these men entered public life.

The Republican party was of course founded on an issue of radical reform: the containment and, as its position eventually developed, the abolition of slavery. This objective was carried out not only through the Civil War and the Emancipation Proclamation, but in succeeding years through the Thirteenth, Fourteenth and Fifteenth Amendments to the Constitution, which in the aggregate were probably the most radical advances in American constitutional government since the founding of the Republic. There followed a period of relative stagnation, brought about largely by too long and too secure a term of office, until the turn of the century when the party came into what undoubtedly stands as its greatest era.

An early indication of what was to follow can be found in the passage in 1890, under the Republican administration of Benjamin Harrison, of the Sherman Anti-Trust Act, which to this day is the cornerstone of the structure of governmental discipline of monopolies. But the full panoply of Republican leadership was reserved for the advent a few years later of six titans whose intellects and energies guided the party and the nation until the party split and lost power in 1912. The first twelve years of the twentieth century were peculiarly the era of Theodore Roosevelt, John Hay, Elihu Root, William Howard Taft, Charles Evans Hughes, and Henry L. Stimson. In those twelve years, this group of six men included two presidents of the United States, one vice president, two governors of New York, two secretaries of state, three secretaries of war, one United States Senator, and one associate justice of the Supreme Court, to say nothing of Hughes's later nomination for the presidency and his tenure as secretary of state and as chief justice, or of Stimson's later tenure as secretary of state and his return, under Franklin Roosevelt, as secretary of war.

In domestic affairs, this Great Era of the Republican party saw the adoption (in the Taft administration) of the federal personal income tax (the Sixteenth Amendment) and the federal corporate income tax, as well as the passage of the Seventeenth Amendment providing for the popular election of senators. In this period the Department of Labor was established and aggressive programs for conservation of natural resources were launched. It was the period of the fight within the party against the great bosses, Platt in New York, Boies Penrose in Pennsylvania, and others, and of the battle for the direct primary as an instrument for transferring party power from the bosses to the people.

In foreign affairs it was the period of Secretary Root's trip around South America—the first such trip by any American Secretary of State; of Roosevelt's leadership in the Treaty of Portsmouth and his participation at the Algeciras Conference; of the building of the Panama Canal; of the sending of the Fleet around the world; of the establishment of constitutional government in Cuba and the Philippines. Whatever one may say about the Republican party in those days, certainly it was lacking neither in imagination nor in leadership. It was neither reactionary at home nor isolationist abroad.

The Republican party was then, as it is now, essentially a conservative party. Its thinking began then, as it does now, with a substantial acceptance of the status quo. But there was a powerful impulse toward such improvements and reforms as could be brought about without risking the basic structure of our govenment and therefore the ultimate usefulness of the reforms themselves. The tendency to reform was not alone a matter of intellectual conviction on the part of men strong both in intellect and conviction, but it had about it a certain *noblesse oblige*. In 1912 Stimson wrote to Theodore Roosevelt: "To me it seems vitally important that the Republican Party, which contains, generally speaking, the richer and more intelligent citizens of the country, should take the lead in reform and not drift into a reactionary position."

Six years before, T.R. had written in similar vein, but in more pungent Roosevelt style, to Philander C. Knox. Unless the Republican party could show "the wage-workers that we are doing justice," he wrote, "we shall some day go down before a radical and extreme democracy with a crash which will be disastrous . . . It would be a dreadful calamity if we saw this country divided into two parties, one containing the bulk of the property owners and conservative people, the other the bulk of the wage-workers and the less prosperous people generally; each party insisting upon demanding much that is wrong, each party sullen and angered by real and fancied grievances. The friends of property, of order, of law . . . must realize that the surest way to provide an explosion of wrong and injustice is to be short-sighted, narrowminded, greedy and arrogant, and to fail to show in actual work that here in this republic it is peculiarly incumbent upon the man with whom things have prospered to be in a certain sense the keeper of his brother with whom life has gone hard."

The same year, defending Roosevelt at a Union League Club dinner from the allegation that he was not "safe," Elihu Root spoke these words:

> He is not safe for the men who wish government to be conducted with greater reference to campaign contributions than to the public good. He is not safe for the men who wish to draw the President of the United States off into a

corner and make whispered arrangements, which they dare
not have known by their constituents. But I say to you that
he has been . . . the greatest conservative force for the
protection of property and our institutions in the city of
Washington. There is a better way to protect property, to
protect capital, to protect great enterprises than by buying
legislatures. There is a better way to deal with labor, and
to keep it from rising into the tumult of the unregulated
and resistless mob than by starving it, or by corrupting its
leaders. That way is, that capital shall be fair . . . fair to
the consumer, fair to the laborer, fair to the investor; that
it shall concede that the laws shall be executed; that its
treatment of the laborer shall be so fair that the reasonable
and more intelligent men among the laborers of our country
shall have their hands held up. . . . Never forget that the
men who labor cast the votes, set up and pull down governments, and that our government is possible, the perpetuity
of our institutions is possible, the continued opportunity for
enterprise, for the enjoyment of wealth, for individual liberty, is possible, only so long as the men who labor with
their hands believe in American liberty and American laws.

Following this period of Republican greatness and vitality
came Woodrow Wilson and World War I. After that there
were eight years of "normalcy" and "business as usual" under
Harding and Coolidge, and in 1929 Herbert Hoover entered
the White House. With his training as an engineer, with his
extraordinarily successful record administering relief in war
devastated post-war Europe and with his eight years experience as secretary of commerce, Hoover was probably one of
the best qualified men in history to assume the presidency.
He was also a man of strong character, high principle, and
dedicated public motivation. However, it was his misfortune
to be president at a time when the United States and the
whole industrial and commercial worlds were struck by the
greatest economic depression of modern history. Hoover did

his best to cope with the problems with which he was confronted, and took a number of courageous and forward looking steps, such as the establishment of the Reconstruction
Finance Corporation. The steps which he took were not
adequate for the need, however, and, in addition, Hoover
lost touch with the overwhelming sentiments of the country on the subject of Prohibition. The result was the election
in 1932 of Franklin D. Roosevelt, after which the Republican
party did not regain the White House until the Eisenhower
presidency twenty years later.

Following the 1932 election, the Republican party went
into opposition in both the upper- and the lower-case sense.
Virtually every Republican leader became convinced that
the New Deal and all its works were the greatest disaster
which ever befell the country. They fought with all their
forces against almost every piece of New Deal reform legislation. Their general attitude can best be recaptured by looking back at the preamble of the 1936 Republican platform.
Party platforms are not noted for their reserve in criticism,
but even by accepted standards the condemnation contained
in the 1936 document was strong. "For three long years," it
said, "the New Deal administration has dishonored American
traditions. . . . The New Deal administration . . . has insisted on the passage of laws contrary to the Constitution.
. . . It has dishonored our country. . . . It has bred fear
and hesitation in commerce and industry. . . . It has secretly made tariff agreements with our foreign competitors,
flooding our markets with foreign commodities. . . . It has
destroyed the morale of many of our people." The last weeks
of the campaign of 1936 were featured in New York by a
daily column which invariably began by pointing out to its
readers how many days then remained "to save the American
Way of Life." Protest against the New Deal program in

those days was absolute, uncompromising, and largely futile.

In foreign affairs the Republican opposition to positions advocated by the president was hardly less violent and more nearly successful. In 1940, in spite of the war in Europe and in spite of the support given to the measure by their own presidential candidate, a majority of Republicans in the Congress voted against the Selective Service Act. In March 1941 a majority in the Senate opposed the Lend-Lease Act, although in the House the Republicans favored it nearly two to one. Eight months later, by a vote of three to one in the Senate and six to one in the House, the Republicans refused to go along with the repeal of the restrictive provisions of the Neutrality Act. In August of that same year, four months before Pearl Harbor, the Republican vote on the extension of Selective Service was in the negative by more than six to one in the House and by nearly two to one in the Senate.

In New York State the political situation between the two world wars was different than at the national level. In 1918 a brilliant young Democratic assemblyman from New York City, Alfred E. Smith, was elected governor. From then through 1938 the Democrats lost the governorship only once, in the Harding landslide of 1920. Even in that landslide, Governor Smith, running for reelection against Nathan Miller, ran a million votes ahead of the national Democratic ticket, and two years later Smith was returned to the Executive Chamber. When Smith was nominated for president in 1928, he was succeeded as governor by Franklin D. Roosevelt, who, prior to his infantile paralysis attack, had been an attractive, anti-organization state senator from Dutchess County, his home in the Hudson Valley. When Roosevelt went to the White House in 1933, he was succeeded by his lieutenant governor, Herbert Lehman, a distinguished banker, humanitarian, and a leader of the Jewish commu-

105

nity, who served until almost the end of 1942, when he resigned to enable his lieutenant governor, Charles Poletti, to occupy the gubernatorial chair for a few short weeks.

In New York City during the same period the mayors had been John F. Hylan and James J. Walker, both organization Democrats. With the city at the brink of financial bankruptcy in 1933, and following a series of highly publicized investigations of political corruption under the leadership of Judge Samuel Seabury, the mayoralty was won by Fiorello H. La Guardia, a colorful and independent figure, who had served several terms as a Republican member of the House of Representatives from the northeastern section of Manhattan, where his constituency included a large part of Harlem and other depressed neighborhoods. Four years earlier, in 1929, he had run unsuccessfully against Walker for mayor. In 1933 La Guardia ran both on the Republican ticket and as a candidate of the Fusion party. The latter party, which was organized for the purpose, provided the mechanism by which large numbers of Democrats and independents, who found it temperamentally and historically difficult to vote for a Republican, were enabled to support him. His regular Democratic opponent was John P. O'Brien, who had been elected to fill out Walker's unexpired term when the latter resigned under pressure. Joseph V. McKee, who had served as mayor for a few months between Walker's resignation and the special election at which O'Brien was elected, was an independent candidate.

In 1937 La Guardia was reelected mayor, this time with the additional support of the American Labor party. The American Labor Party had been founded the year before by a number of prominent labor leaders, including Sidney Hillman, David Dubinsky, and Jacob Potofsky. The formation of the ALP had been encouraged by President Roosevelt, who was running for reelection that year, and who saw it as a vehicle to enhance his majority in that campaign. A number of leaders in the regular Democratic organization in the state had significant reservations concerning the creation of this new political vehicle, fearing that it would not limit its activities to the 1936 campaign, but would take on a life of its own in later years. This, of course, was exactly what happened and, as indicated, the ALP support was a critical part of La Guardia's reelection victory in 1937, as it was again in 1941 when he was elected to a third term. As a consequence, while La Guardia remained nominally a Republican, his actual identification with the Republican organization and with Republican philosophy diminished as his term of office progressed. Indeed, by the end of his second term his relationship with the ALP and with the Democratic national administration in Washington, together with the personal following engendered by his colorful leadership, provided his true political base.

This, then, was the historical perspective and the political situation when, in the early 1930s, young Tom Dewey strode out onto the political stage.

II

The appointment of Thomas E. Dewey as special rackets prosecutor was due, in large part, to George Z. Medalie, a prominent and influential New York attorney, whose assistant Dewey had been from 1931 to 1933 when Medalie was United States attorney for the Southern District of New York. A growth in racketeering unusual even for the city of New York had created the need for such an appointment, and Governor Lehman was persuaded by Medalie of the wisdom of appointing somebody from the opposing political party.

At the time Dewey was only thirty-three years old. He was born in Owosso, Michigan, and had graduated from the University of Michigan and Columbia Law School. After six years in private practice in New York City, he was appointed in 1931 as Medalie's assistant, in which post he served for two years, and during the last part of his term he succeeded briefly to the top position in that office. Thereafter, he returned to private practice and in 1935 received the rackets appointment, the technical title of which was Special Prosecutor, Investigation of Organized Crime. Dewey did an outstanding job as special prosecutor. He secured significant convictions of prominent and colorful members of the underworld, and the resulting publicity made him one of the best known persons of his age in the United States.

In 1937 Dewey ran for the office of district attorney of New York County on the same ticket as La Guardia and won. The following year he obtained the Republican nomination for governor, but was defeated by Herbert H. Lehman. Two years later, still only thirty-eight years old and having held no elective office except that of district attorney, Dewey became a serious candidate for president. Although he lost the nomination to Wendell Willkie, he received more votes on the first ballot than any other candidate at the Philadelphia convention. Following Willkie's nomination, he offered to be of help in the ensuing campaign, and he turned over to Willkie's people all his lists of volunteers and other supporters. Willkie never felt warmly toward Dewey, however, and did not avail himself of Dewey's offer to any significant degree.

In 1942 Dewey was again nominated for governor. The Democrats, under the leadership of James J. Farley, nominated John F. Bennet, Jr., an organization man, to oppose him. This was not received warmly by the wing of the party which looked for its leadership to President Roosevelt rather than to Farley, however, and many of such persons supported Dean Alfange, who was the candidate of the American Labor party. With the Democrats thus divided, Dewey won the election, and the Executive Mansion passed into the hands of the Republicans for the first time in twenty years.

In 1944 Dewey achieved the Republican nomination for president but lost the election to Franklin D. Roosevelt, who was elected to his fourth term and who died shortly thereafter. In 1946 Dewey was reelected to the governorship by a very large majority. Then in 1948 came his famous defeat for the presidency by Harry S. Truman.

Of all Dewey's accomplishments in life, it has always seemed to me that one of the most outstanding was the philosophical way in which he took this startling setback to his ambitions and his career. The desire to be president is an infection of great power and many strong men have been warped by its denial. The lives of Theodore Roosevelt, Al Smith, and Wendell Willkie were all deeply marked by their loss of the presidency. Dewey, on the other hand, returned to his duties as governor of New York and then later to private life without any visible signs of bitterness or disillusion, and lived out twenty more years of useful and constructive existence in the practice of the law and with his family.

Because of the circumstances of his defeat in 1948, Dewey had perhaps more reason than most other unsuccessful candidates to be embittered. What made his defeat so startling, of course, was that all the indications prior to election day were that he would win easily. President Truman appeared to have lost control not only of the country but even of his own party. The extreme right wing of his party, located mostly in the south, was in substantial revolt against his civil rights program. The extreme left wing deserted the party for Henry Wallace, who ran for president independently as the candidate of the Progressive party. All the polls indicated a sweeping Dewey victory. Indeed, the story is that when the governor and his closest supporters gathered for dinner on election night in the house on East 93rd Street of Roger W. Straus, one of his warm friends, the principal item on the agenda was a discussion of possible appointees to the cabinet.

Why Dewey lost in 1948 and why Truman won is a matter upon which experts have never agreed and never will. The American public tends to like the underdog, but that can hardly be the whole explanation. Maybe it was that Dewey was overconfident, and that this overconfidence tended to exaggerate a personality which was somewhat stiff and remote at best. Maybe it was that the Great Depression for which the Republicans under President Hoover had been generally, if largely unfairly, given the blame, was still too close to the voters' memories for them to want to trust a Republican with the White House. In any event, Truman won and in his second term achieved a record which secured for him a place in history, if not as one of our great presidents, certainly as one of our very good ones.

Following his defeat for the presidency, Dewey resumed his duties as governor of New York and in 1950 was elected to a third term. He almost certainly could have been elected again in 1954, but he chose instead to retire to private life. The nomination went that year to Irving Ives, who had been elected to the United States Senate in the Dewey landslide of 1946 after a distinguished career as a member of the Assembly. Ives waged a singularly ineffective campaign, however, and was narrowly defeated by Averell Harriman. In the closing days of the campaign Governor Dewey took to the television in a valiant effort to turn the tide, but was not successful.

III

In the late 1930s and the early 1940s the Young Republican Club of New York was an active and, as such organizations go, a reasonably effective group. Made up largely but not entirely of young lawyers, it sponsored a series of weekly lunches at which persons of prominence were asked to speak, and it took public positions on issues of importance. When election time came around, the club usually concentrated its efforts behind a few selected candidates, thus magnifying the effectiveness of its manpower. Dewey was a member of the club and his campaigns, beginning with his campaign for district attorney, were always high on the club's list of priorities. As a result, the members of the club, of which I was one, had the opportunity of knowing Dewey and of working with him. In the period immediately following World War II, I had the opportunity of getting to know him even better.

Following his defeat in 1944, Dewey's program called for reelection as governor in 1946 and then a new try for the White House in 1948. By 1946 Willkie had been dead two years, but his mystique, always great, was more powerful in memory even than it had been in life. It was natural that Dewey wanted, insofar as possible, to augment his own strength by gathering some of that mystique to his cause. He concluded, because of my association with Willkie, that I could be of help to that end.

Accordingly, during the early part of 1946 I had the pleasure of a number of visits with the governor. On one occasion I rode with him on the train from New York to Albany and on others I saw him in the apartment in the Roosevelt Hotel where he maintained his New York City headquarters or in his office in the Capitol in Albany. The most pleasant circumstance in which I saw him was when he

111

invited me to his annual dinner at the Executive Mansion for the members of the Court of Appeals, New York's highest court. The governor pointed out to me that that dinner was the most prestigious of the official season, and a very enjoyable evening it was for a youngish lawyer just resuming his practice after the war.

My discussions with the governor focused mainly on two subjects. The first involved the possibility of my organizing some sort of citizens' group, perhaps on the order of the Willkie clubs, which would help revitalize the Republican party in New York City. Because the voter registration in the city was so preponderantly in favor of the Democrats, the Republican organization was hopelessly weak, with the exception of a few isolated areas, such as the east side of Manhattan. Indeed, it was a notorious fact that the Republican leaders in many cases survived largely by crumbs which they gathered from the table of their colleagues in the Democratic organization. As a consequence, the objective of many Republican leaders was much more to maintain their positions of leadership within the party than it was to strengthen the party at election time. Perceiving this, Dewey was looking for some vehicle which would either stimulate the Republican leaders into greater activity or would supplement them with an undertaking whose objective would be victory instead of mere survival. I made an effort to put such a group together and, on one occasion, the governor gathered a number of the leaders of the organization to hear my views. It was one thing to accomplish an objective of this kind during campaign time, however, and quite another to accomplish it between campaigns. In any case, the effort was not successful and in due course I regretfully so informed the governor.

The other matter which we discussed at our meetings was the possibility of my joining his administration. The first sug-

Wendell Willkie and the author in 1940 election eve broadcast.

High command of Willkie campaign at meeting in Colorado Springs, Colorado. *Left to right, front:* Samuel F. Pryor, Joseph W. Martin, Jr., Willkie, John D. Hamilton, Henry Fletcher. *Back:* Russell Davenport, Charles E. Goodspeed, the author, Harold E. Stassen, Sinclair Weeks.

Author's father as a young man, and pencil sketch of author's mother by Helleu.

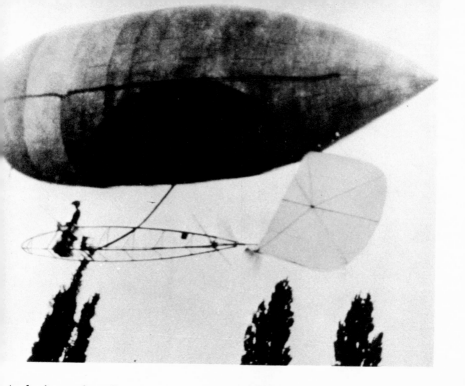

Author's mother flying over Bois de Boulogne in Santos Dumont's airship Number Nine.

Author's mother with Santos Dumont.

Vice Admiral Jonas H. Ingram.

Rear Admiral Alan G. Kirk.

Author with Captain Clinton E. Braine, Admiral Ingram's chief of staff.

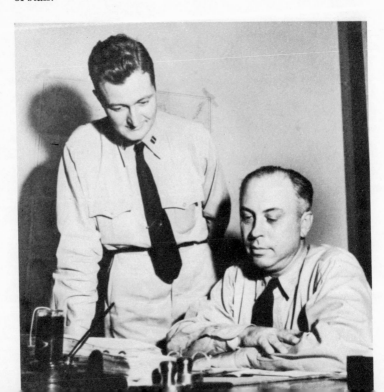

Author in naval uniform with his sister, Alva (Mrs. Charles F. Bound).

Governor Rockefeller with Oren Root, Mrs. Root, and three of their four children.

Author and his two oldest sons with Pope John XXIII.

Oren Root.

gestion was that I become a member of the New York State Power Authority. This entity, to which the governor had the power of appointment, was very close to his heart, since he was a great believer in the future of public power and also of the St. Lawrence Seaway, which was then in the early stages of development. Membership on the Power Authority was a part-time undertaking but paid a salary which was generous in the circumstances. For a young lawyer with few clients and little financial means it was an attractive offer. But for me there was a hitch.

The hitch for me arose out of the fact that, even though he was dead, I still felt an overriding loyalty to Wendell Willkie and to the things for which he stood. Rightly or wrongly, Willkie had never had a high regard for Dewey. He suspected him of acting more out of opportunity than out of principle, and was especially suspicious of Dewey's reliability in the area of international cooperation. Because of my loyalty to Willkie's memory, I did not wish to put myself in a position which would restrict my freedom to support somebody other than Dewey for the 1948 nomination should I wish to do so, and I felt that acceptance of a post in his administration would so restrict me.

Accordingly, I turned the governor down. Because I did not want to be entirely frank as to my reasons, it was not an easy thing to do, and I had to plead ignorance in the field of power regulation as my excuse. Thereafter, he offered me a position on the Law Revision Commission, which, while perhaps not as influential as the Power Authority, was nevertheless an interesting assignment. This was even harder to turn down, but turn it down I did. I am not sure that at my present stage in life I would be so quixotic, but at the age of thirty-five that is the way I felt. I admired Dewey and respected him, but I wanted to retain my freedom of action. In retrospect I think I should have been more frank with him and I am confident he would have respected me if I had. On another occasion, when Senator Taft asked for my political support for the presidential nomination in 1952, I did tell him frankly that I could not give it.

The final offer from the governor was the most interesting of all. The seat in the Seventeenth Congressional District in Manhattan had for many years been safe for the Republicans. For a time it had been occupied by Ruth Baker Pratt, a lady of energy and distinction as well as of wealth, and in 1946 it was occupied by Joseph Clark Baldwin. Joe Baldwin was a gentleman of great charm and polish. I knew him well and had gone to school with two of his younger brothers. In the later years of his congressional service, Baldwin tended a little too much in the liberal direction to suit the tastes of the leaders of the Republican organization in Manhattan. He might have survived his liberal inclinations, however, if he had not at the same time become slightly lax in his attention to his congressional duties.

In any event, the decision was reached in the Republican high command that the party would be strengthened if somebody younger and more vigorous were to take Joe Baldwin's place. It was thus that one day I received a telephone call from one of the senior members of Governor Dewey's staff asking me on behalf of the governor if I would be willing to run in the Republican primary against Baldwin. I was assured of the full support of the organization, which in that district had some vitality. Indeed, there did not seem to be much doubt that any reasonably competent person could take the nomination away from Baldwin and, since the district was safely Republican in those days, the nomination would be tantamount to election.

This was, of course, tempting. However, I turned that down, too, both for the reason that I had turned down the two earlier suggestions and also because I could not bring myself to be the instrument by which Joe Baldwin, whom I liked, was sent to oblivion. As events turned out, State Senator Frederic R. Coudert was chosen to do the job, which he did effectively and without too much trouble.

There then came a time when Governor Dewey had it in his power to give me something which I could accept. That was the 1946 nomination for the United States Senate. I suppose it could be said that my willingness to accept that nomination from his hands proves that every man has his price and that I was a hypocrite in pretending that my earlier refusals had been based on principle. That was not my view, however. My view was that as an appointive member of a state agency, or even as one of a considerable number of Republican members of the House of Representatievs from New York, I would have very limited freedom of political action as a practical matter. On the other hand, as a member of the United States Senate I would be on a level of near equality with the governor himself, and my views would have to be reckoned with. Since my reservations with respect to Dewey arising out of my Willkie relationship were not to his person but to his potential policy positions, it seemed to me that a seat in the Senate would further my principles rather than compromise them. As it turned out, of course, I did not get the nomination, so that my judgment as to what would be the effect of my getting it was never put to the test.

The whole matter arose because of the potential candidacy for that same nomination of General William J. Donovan, a colorful lawyer who during World War II had headed the Office of Strategic Services. Donovan, who had considerable political connections, was organizing a campaign directed toward forcing the hands of the governor and the state Republican leaders and thereby achieving the nomination. Dewey was not happy about having Donovan as the senatorial candidate and was casting about for a substitute. In those days religious and ethnic matters carried more weight in the construction of political tickets than they do today. Since Donovan was a Catholic, Dewey concluded that he should, if possible, find a Catholic with whom to stop him. He settled upon Hugh A. Drum, a retired general, who headed the State Guard and was also a Catholic. Drum's candidacy did not meet with much enthusiasm around the state, however, and it appeared that the governor might have some difficulty in heading Donovan off. It was at that moment, remembering the various offers which had been made to me, that I concluded that maybe I, especially since I was a Catholic, might have a chance to get the nomination. Because it appeared that Dewey would almost certainly sweep to victory at the head of the ticket the following November, as indeed he did, the nomination would be the equivalent of election.

It was not necessary for me to advance my own name, because there are always good friends willing to do that sort of thing for an aspiring candidate. In this instance the good friend was John A. Wells, a fellow member of the New York Young Republican Club with whom I was then on good terms and with whom my friendship has grown and developed over the years. Jack Wells launched my candidacy with a carefully drawn letter to a number of important Republican leaders in the state. In at least a few quarters it met with a warm response, enough to encourage me to make some efforts of my own. In this last connection. I remember especially an evening with McGeorge Bundy in a guest house belonging to Henry L. Stimson on Long Island. Bundy, with whom I had served as a member of Admiral Kirk's staff in the invasion of Normandy, was in the process of writing Stimson's biography, and I was spending the weekend with him. My particular recollection is the effort which he and I made to reach Mrs. Ogden Reid on the telephone at her Adirondack hideaway on Upper St. Regis Lake. The purpose of our effort was to prevail upon Mrs. Reid, whose husband was the owner and publisher of the *Herald Tribune,* to place an editorial in that paper in support of my candidacy. I cannot recall whether or not we reached her. If we did, I am sure she did what she could, since she was always a good friend.

In the end the whole effort came to nothing. Governor Dewey invited me one day to his rooms in the Roosevelt, where he was more frank with me than I on earlier occasions had been with him, although even then he did not tell me the whole story, and to this day I do not know it. What he told me was that he was sure that I would make a good candidate and a good senator, and that, if elected, I would probably stay in the Senate for many years. But he added that he was not going to give me the nomination and that I might as well forget it. Whether this was because he, too, had figured out that a United States senator can be an independent person to be reckoned with and that he did not want to reckon with me at that level, I do not know. Maybe it was simply that he had already found a satisfactory alternative to Donovan. As indicated in an earlier part of this chapter, the person who received the nomination and went on to win the election was Irving Ives, a distinguished member of the Assembly.

IV

In 1949 the mayor of New York City was William O'Dwyer, a Democrat who had been elected to that office four years earlier over Judge Jonah Goldstein, the Republican-Fusion candidate. The nominee who had been selected by the leaders of the Republican party and the Liberal party to oppose O'Dwyer in 1949 was Newbold Morris, a highly principled but somewhat stiff patrician who had been president of the City Council under La Guardia. The Liberal party was flushed with success at that moment, since in May of that year Franklin D. Roosevelt, Jr., in a special election running on the Liberal ticket alone, had been elected to a congressional seat from the west side of Manhattan.

In the course of the summer of 1949 I was approached by Thomas J. Curran, the Republican county chairman of New York County, who offered me the nomination for the relatively minor office of president of the borough of Manhattan. That office was occupied at the moment by Hugo E. Rogers, who was the leader of the Manhattan Democratic organization, known as Tammany Hall. It appeared that he would be a vulnerable target. It also appeared that he would have no attraction to the Liberal party, so that there should be a good likelihood of my getting that party's endorsement. While I realized that my chances of winning the election were a good deal less than fifty-fifty, even with the Liberal endorsement, I nevertheless thought it was worth the try and I accepted Curran's offer.

What happened after that is something which I suppose I should take as a compliment. Mayor O'Dwyer, having read in the papers of my selection by the Republican leaders and foreseeing that the Liberal party might very well give me its nomination as well, arranged for the withdrawal of Rogers as a candidate and the substitution of Robert F. Wagner, Jr. Wagner was the attractive and respected son of a much revered father. At the time he was chairman of the City Planning Commission and had previously been commissioner of Housing and Buildings under O'Dwyer. Wagner also was close to the leaders of the Liberal party, both through his father and in his own right. Accordingly, the

118

moment that the substitution took place my chances for the Liberal endorsement went out the window. Simultaneously, any slight chance I might have had of winning the election went out the window as well. In spite of this unexpected and damaging turn of events, I concluded that I was morally bound to accept the Republican endorsement and to make the hopeless race. I convinced myself that even if I had no chance of winning, I could have some fun and perhaps contribute in some small degree to the public welfare by airing the issues.

There is no doubt that I did enjoy the campaign, the more so because, since there was no chance of winning, I did not have to carefully weigh every word and act but could say what I thought was right, irrespective of the consequences. One of the problems, of course, was to get any publicity, especially since I was running for a relatively minor and subordinate office. At that time Robert Moses was the very colorful commissioner of parks of New York City. I quickly found that one way to get myself into the headlines was to engage in controversy with Moses. Since Moses was a talented and unusually effective public servant, it was not easy to find an issue with which to engage him. However, I learned that the Department of Parks was proposing to spend several hundred thousands of dollars in the erection of the statues of two South American statesmen at the head of the Avenue of the Americas. In one of my public speeches I raised the question of whether, in the light of the desperate need for money for schools, playgrounds, hospitals, and housing, the money being expended on the statues might not be better spent otherwise.

The account of my speech was buried away in small print on the inside of the newspapers. It was not so buried, however, that Moses did not see it. The commissioner issued a blast at me, couched in his usual purple prose, which was promptly reported in large headlines. Thereafter, I made a counter-reply, which again appeared in the back of the papers. To my very great satisfaction Moses then felt obliged to issue still another blast, which for the second time put me in the headlines. This little story should be concluded with the fact that my public interchanges with Moses in no way marred my personal relationship with him. Indeed, when I ran into him a few months later at a dinner of the Inner Circle, which is an organization of political newspaper men, I hailed him "good evening, General Bolivar," and got a warm handshake and a big smile in return.

One of the small footnotes to history which should perhaps be recorded concerning my campaign for borough president was that, to the best of my knowledge, I was the first political candidate ever to use television. Television in 1949 was in its infancy and only a small fraction of the voters had yet acquired a set. Nevertheless, since I was so much less well-known than my opponent, I decided to try it. Accordingly, I committed a substantial part of my meager campaign funds for fifteen minutes a week on the local NBC station. On those programs I gathered groups of citizens of various points of view who interrogated me and gave me an opportunity to project my own opinions. There is no reason to believe that this very modest use of that medium had any significant effect upon the number of votes which I received, but I have always been proud of the fact that I pioneered a campaign device which in later years was to become so overwhelmingly important.

Since those early days, I have given a good deal of thought to the use of television in political campaigns, and I have come to see a number of dangers in it. There is, of course, the matter of its very great expense and the consequent advantage to a well-financed candidate over a less well-financed one. But there are other dangers, too. For example, it is possible for a candidate to tape a show, with one or two hours of tape being cut to fifteen or twenty minutes or so. The resulting presentation has the appearance of a live show, whereas in fact all the tell-tale mistakes and blunders which would reveal the candidate's weaknesses have been eliminated. To be sure, in such a situation the fact that the show was taped would be disclosed, but the full import of that disclosure would not necessarily be understood by the average viewer. Two offsets against the dangers of such a "canned" presentation are the unrehearsed television debate and the unrehearsed television interview. I trust that both of these devices will continue to be part of important campaigns.

The Republican candidate for senator in 1949 was John Foster Dulles, who had been appointed to fill the vacancy caused by the resignation on account of illness of Senator Wagner. I recall an occasion when I was down on the waterfront with my sound truck addressing a group of longshoremen at their "shape-up," which was the crude circumstance in which these men had to seek employment in those days. As I was talking, Senator Dulles drove by. Seeing what was going on, he stopped and asked whether he could share my simple facilities. Needless to say, I was much honored to make them available to so distinguished a public figure.

There is an amusing story about John Foster Dulles which may be appropriate to tell at this point. My law school classmate, Edwin Cohen, who later became my law partner and ultimately became undersecretary of the treasury in the administration of President Nixon, started his law career as an associate with Sullivan & Cromwell, of which Dulles was then the senior partner. Lawyers in large New York City law firms ordinarily arrive at work between 9:30 and a quarter of ten in the morning. However, on the first day of his employment Cohen was so anxious to be on time that he arrived shortly after nine o'clock. As he emerged from the elevator on the floor on which Sullivan & Cromwell was located, an older man who had been with him in the elevator inquired as to his name. Having learned that he was a new associate of the office, the older man introduced himself as John Foster Dulles. The very next day Cohen's suburban train broke down, with the result that he did not arrive at the office until after ten o'clock. By strange coincidence his companion in the elevator was again Mr. Dulles. As they emerged from the elevator that morning, the great man turned to Cohen and said "young man, you learn quickly."

The mayoralty that year was won by O'Dwyer and Herbert Lehman defeated Dulles for the Senate. Needless to say, Robert Wagner won the presidency of the borough of Manhattan by a very large margin and went on at a later time to become mayor. My regard for Wagner has been much heightened by the fact that since that campaign, in the course of which I said many of the harsh things that one normally says about one's opponent, he has nevertheless maintained an unfailingly warm and friendly attitude toward me.

V

The accomplishments of Thomas E. Dewey's long governorship were many. One, certainly, was his careful and responsible fiscal policy. Although many social programs were inaugurated and developed under his leadership, he always treated the public's money as if it were his own. He scrupulously guarded the surpluses which were developed during the war period, when many programs had to be deferred, even to the point of trying in legitimate ways to hide them in his budget from the eyes of the legislature. The great New

York Thruway, which was later named for him and which was the first major toll road of its kind in the country, is another significant accomplishment. But for me the two outstanding achievements of Dewey's governorship were the creation of the State Commission Against Discrimination and his enormously constructive influence upon the judiciary.

The New York State legislature had been addressing itself in piecemeal fashion to the subject of discrimination for many years. As early as 1909 the state prohibited discrimination because of race, creed, or color in such areas as jury service, the right to practice law, admissions to public schools, and in other areas. During World War II there were governmental committees on discrimination designed to minimize discrimination against minorities, especially in areas relating to the war effort. However, it was not until 1944, with the creation by the legislature of the New York State Temporary Commission Against Discrimination, that the possibility of extending the jurisdiction of the state to discrimination in general began to take concrete form. The Temporary Commission held hearings throughout the state and rendered its report in January 1945. In his message to the legislature that year, the governor strongly urged that the report become the basis for legislation "to place our state in the forefront of the nation in the handling of this vital issue."

As a result of the report of the Temporary Commission and of the governor's message, a bill was introduced into the legislature by Assembly Majority Leader Irving M. Ives and Senate Minority Leader Elmer F. Quinn. The bill became law a few months later. It prohibited discrimination because of race, creed, color, or national origin by employers of six or more persons and set up a permanent State Commission Against Discrimination to effect its provisions. Viewed in retrospect, the bill was only a very small beginning, because while it gave the commission some sanctions, it relied heavily on education and persuasion. It is hard today, with all that has been accomplished since, to realize what a big step forward that was, but at the time it was a major trail-blazing effort.

The controversy surrounding this kind of legislation became even clearer two years later, when an effort was made under the leadership of Senator Ives, who by that time had gone to the United States Senate, to pass a comparable bill at the federal level. At the request of A. Philip Randolph, the very great president of the International Brotherhood of Sleeping Car Porters, I undertook to try to develop some support for that federal legislation. Since it already had the support of leading church groups and civil rights groups, it occurred to me that the most useful thing for me to do might be to organize some support in the business community.

Accordingly, I set out to put together a committee of businessmen for that purpose. I was able to get fourteen signatures of persons of prominence to a telegram which was dispatched to Joseph Martin, the Speaker of the House of Representatives, and to Senator Vandenberg, the President pro tempore of the Senate. It is interesting to note, however, that I had to ask more than sixty individuals in order to get fourteen signatories. The others either declined to join or did not reply. Those who signed the telegram, in addition to myself, were William L. Batt, president, S.K.F. Industries; Allen W. Dulles, a partner of Sullivan & Cromwell; Paul G. Hoffman, president, Studebaker Corporation; Eric Johnston, president, Motion Picture Association; Henry R. Luce, of Time, Inc.; Dwight R. G. Palmer, president, General Cable Corporation; Martin Quigley, president, Quigley Publishing Co.; Nelson A. Rockefeller; Anna M. Rosenberg, a well-known public relations person who later became Assistant Secretary of Defense for Manpower during World War II;

Beardsley Ruml, chairman of the board, R. H. Macy & Co.; Spyros P. Skouras, president, Twentieth Century-Fox Film Corporation; Paul C. Smith, general manager, San Francisco Chronicle; Herbert Bayard Swope, the well-known publicist; and Charles H. Tuttle, a partner of Breed, Abbott & Morgan. It is interesting to note that two of the signers of the telegram later married: fourteen years later Anna Rosenberg became Mrs. Paul Hoffman.

While Senator Ives's bill did not pass the Congress, it was reported out favorably by the Senate Committee on Labor and Public Welfare, which constituted the first time that any comparable bill had been favorably acted upon by a Senate committee. In that connection there is an interesting story relating to Senator Robert A. Taft of Ohio. While Senator Taft was more progressive in some areas than was generally understood, especially in the areas of federal aid to housing, health, and education, he was in the main a very conservative person. Indeed, at the national Republican convention in 1952 at which Eisenhower was nominated, he led the conservative opposition to that nomination. Because he was an important member of the Senate Committee on Labor and Public Welfare, a group of us visited him in connection with the pending legislation.

The senator gave our group a thorough and courteous hearing, in the course of which he displayed a considerable sympathy at least for the objectives of the pending legislation, if not for its details. On returning to New York, I wrote him a letter of thanks and told him what a favorable impression he had made upon the group. Almost anybody else would have left the matter there, but not Senator Taft. So concerned was he that we might have overestimated his support for the legislation that he replied to my letter with a letter of his own, expressing the hope that he had not created the impression that he was in favor of the bill since in

fact he was not. He added, however, that in spite of his opposition, he would nevertheless do everything he could to
bring the bill to a vote in his committee. As indicated above,
not only did it come to a vote, but the committee approved
it. A lesser man would have been happy to have been a little
vague and to have allowed us to believe that he was somewhat more for the bill than he was in fact. But Senator Taft
was too highly principled for that. Indeed, this little story
tells a good deal about him.

Of all the areas on which Governor Dewey left his mark,
however, the one which perhaps has been the most enduring
is the judiciary. Dewey loved the law. He was not a man of
strongly professed formal religion, and in some ways the law
was his religion. His early success, of course, was in the law
and in the course of that success he developed a staff of able
men, many of whom ended up, either by his direct or in-
direct intervention, on the bench. Included among the
judges who began their careers with him or who owed their
appointment or election, directly or indirectly, to him, or
both, are Stanley Fuld, until recently the chief judge of the
New York State Court of Appeals and Charles D. Breitel, a
distinguished member of that court who is fully qualified to
succeed Judge Fuld; David W. Peck, who for many years
was a highly effective presiding justice of the Appellate Division for the First Department; J. Edward Lumbard, for
many years the chief judge of the United States Court of
Appeals for the Second Circuit and still a senior judge of
that court; Murray I. Gurfein, Arnold Bauman, Whitman
Knapp, and the late Edward C. McLean, all judges of the
United States District Court for the Second Circuit, and William H. Timbers, chief judge of the United States District
Court for Connecticut. Others include Jacob Grumet, a justice of the New York Supreme Court, First Judicial District;
Florence Kelley, administrative judge of the Family Court;

126

and William T. Mertens, a judge of the Civil Court. In addition in 1943 Dewey appointed Francis E. Rivers to the City Court of the City of New York which, in spite of its name, was a state court. The significance of that appointment, strange as it may seem today, lay in the fact that Judge Rivers was the first Negro ever to sit as a New York State judge.

One of the impressive aspects of Dewey's record with respect to the judiciary is that many of the individuals who began their legal careers with him or who owe their appointments to him are still sitting on the bench, so that the governor's influence continues to be felt through them nearly twenty years after he left the Executive Chamber. Moreover, his influence extended indirectly even outside of the state of New York and of the federal courts located in the state. From 1953 to 1960 the attorneys general of the United States were successively Herbert Brownell and William P. Rogers, both close and early associates of Dewey. In addition, Lawrence E. Walsh, who had served with Dewey in the New York County District Attorney's Office and was his counsel for a time when he was governor, served for three of those years as deputy attorney general. In that period many significant appointments were made to the federal courts around the country, including the appointment in 1955 of the late John M. Harlan to the Supreme Court of the United States, the appointment in 1957 of John Minor Wisdom to the Circuit Court for the Fifth Circuit, and the appointment the following year of Potter Stewart to the Supreme Court. Brownell, Rogers, and Walsh were in a position to be influential with respect to such appointments. It is not stretching matters very far, therefore, to say that that influence in turn reflected the training and point of view of Governor Dewey.

After his second defeat for the presidency, Dewey returned to his first love, the law, where he carved out a new and highly successful career. In 1952 he played a major role in rallying the country's Republican governors in support of Eisenhower's nomination, and thereafter he was always available for consultation by those carrying the burdens of public office. But mainly he practiced law, which was where he had started, until his untimely death in 1971.

CHAPTER FIVE

Post-War Politics in New York State— The Later Years

I

It has been my observation that there are few greater liabilities that a person can carry in life than too much money, too much good looks, or too much personal charm. History, including modern history, is full of persons who, because they put excessive reliance upon one or another of those gifts, came a cropper in the end. Nelson Rockefeller rose above not one or two but all three of these potential liabilities and turned them into assets. Of his personal fortune, one of the largest in the history of the world, he is quoted as having said that he never found it a hardship to be a Rockefeller. His manly good looks, his warm and gregarious personality, together with his money, have for him been tools to accomplish the goals which he found important. It is the good fortune of his fellow countrymen that those goals, by and large, have been the public interest.

Rockefeller has also deeply believed in his lucky star, and in most cases this has not let him down. As he flies around the country in one or another of the Rockefeller family planes, there are those who say he seems to command the elements. Other planes may be halted or delayed by mechanical problems, scheduling problems, or weather, but as the governor's plane waits to take off or to land, the clouds seem to part just long enough for him to get through. A further example of his good luck is a story told by his first wife, Mary Todhunter Clark Rockefeller. According to that story, after the birth of their first three children there was disagreement between husband and wife as to whether they should have one more child or two, she favoring one and he two. As it turned out the last progeny of that marriage were twins, thus giving him his way without need for further discussion.

Another of Rockefeller's outstanding characteristics is a belief that, given the right mixture of organization, effort, determination, and money, there is nothing which cannot be accomplished. The Albany Mall is an example. When the old, Victorian Executive Mansion on Eagle Street in Albany was badly damaged by fire during his first term, many persons advocated its abandonment. The neighborhood surrounding the mansion had deteriorated over the years, and it seemed to many that the fire provided a perfect opportunity to move the gubernatorial residence to a more attractive suburban location. But these people did not know Nelson Rockefeller. Not only did he cause the old mansion to be rebuilt and refurbished, but, in part at his own expense, he added new facilities, including a tennis court and, more recently, a swimming pool. More importantly, with a gesture worthy of Cosimo de Medici, he decreed that if the neighborhood in which the mansion found itself was bad, the remedy was not to move the mansion but to change the neighborhood. The result was the total razing of a vast area surrounding the mansion, leaving nothing standing except that building and the Roman Catholic Cathedral next door. In place of all that was razed there was to rise in due course the great complex of government buildings known as the Albany Mall.

The government of the city of Albany has been controlled during modern times by the O'Connell machine. Founded by Ed O'Connell and headed in later years by his brother, Dan, the machine has had all the virtues and all the vices of the old-fashioned, paternalistic organizations which were common in large cities in earlier times and of which it is one of the last surviving examples. The O'Connells believed in the simple virtues of home, neighborhood, church, and one-to-one personal loyalty. Public housing, urban redevelopment, and similar projects were regarded as newfangled, semi-socialistic enterprises, calculated to break down long-established groupings and to attract unreliable and undesirable new residents. As a consequence, Albany through the years became an increasingly backward city, economically, socially and intellectually. A succession of governors sought to change the situation. Governor Dewey mounted a major assault upon the machine, but without significant results. It took Nelson Rockefeller with his Mall to accomplish with imagination, money, and persuasion at least part of what earlier governors had failed to accomplish by confrontation and force.

The Mall has of course had its problems, and these have

131

been well publicized. But it has gone forward and it will be completed. When it is finished, it will be one of the most beautiful and impressive government complexes in the world. When that time comes, all the travail, all the extra cost will be forgotten, and Nelson Rockefeller will have lived up to the characterization given him as "the best mayor Albany ever had." It will also add one more monument to the incredible list of monuments for which New York can thank, in whole or in part, the leadership and generosity of the Rockefeller family. These include, in addition to Rockefeller Center and the Albany Mall, the Riverside Church and the Cloisters, both on Riverside Drive; the United Nations complex; Lincoln Center for the Performing Arts; the Chase Manhattan Bank building; the twin towers of the World Trade Center; and the many vast campuses of the State University of New York, whose staunchest friend and supporter has been Nelson Rockefeller. Although they are more a monument of nature than of man, there should perhaps also be included the stately Palisades on the western shore of the Hudson River estuary, which long ago were purchased and donated to the public by John D. Rockefeller, Jr., thus preserving them forever from the depredations of private developers.

II

My first acquaintance with Rockefeller was at a very young age at the Lincoln School, which was then located on Park Avenue between 66th and 67th Streets in New York City, and was one of the early schools experimenting in progressive education. The Rockefeller family supported what the school was trying to accomplish, and their three middle sons, Nelson, Laurence and Winthrop, were students there at the time that I was also a student in grades one to three. I recall all three Rockefeller boys, and I also hold a mental picture of their mother calling for them from time to time in one of those high, square, electrically propelled motor cars, which, because of their peculiar shape, were known as "hat boxes." My memory of Nelson, who was three years older than I, is of a boy who even at that age was attractive and dynamic, already showing to his teachers and fellow students the qualities of leadership which became apparent to all in later years.

During the early 1930s, after his graduation from Dartmouth, Rockefeller played a major role in the operations of Rockefeller Center, across the street from St. Patrick's Cathedral in New York City, which had been built with great courage and imagination by his father in the depths of the depression. During that same period my mother was chairman of the Municipal Art Committee, an organization which came into being under the patronage of Mayor La Guardia, with a view to giving some artistic direction to the many public works and relief projects which he, together with President Roosevelt's administration in Washington, were bringing to life in New York City. It was natural that my mother should seek the advice and support of the young millionaire who was directing a major real estate operation in mid-Manhattan. Thus, the contact between my family and Nelson Rockefeller was resumed, and my mother was always grateful for the kindness and encouragement which she received from that source.

My own personal contacts with Nelson Rockefeller were renewed as a consequence of my effort for Wendell Willkie. In the spring of 1940 our effort to develop support for Willkie's nomination was staffed by volunteers and operated very much on a shoestring, with small contributions coming in, mostly from people who were relatively unknown. This was so partly because we had no other choice, and partly also because the effectiveness of what we were trying to do depended in some measure, at least in those early days, upon projecting an image of simplicity, naiveté, and lack of funds.

In the light of the above, the reader will understand the impact upon our small effort when one morning there came a note from Nelson Rockefeller enclosing a personal contribution. I do not today recall the exact amount of his check, but my best recollection is that it was for $2,000. The exact amount is not important in any case, because the point of the story is that it was for an amount very many times larger than the largest contribution which had been received by my office up to that moment. At first my colleagues' and my reaction was one of elation. Upon further reflection, however, we began to worry about the possible effect of such a contribution upon our public image. While $2,000 was not a large sum for Rockefeller, and while it was not large by comparison with other political contributions, even in those days, it was very large by the standards of our simple, volunteer effort.

After consultation within the office, the decision was made to return to Rockefeller a part of his contribution. This was a delicate matter, however, because I was touched and grateful for his support and did not wish to offend him. It seemed unwise, therefore, to return it to him by mail. Accordingly, I got him on the telephone and asked to see him. Believing quite naturally that my purpose was to seek a larger contribution, he sought to put me off. The conversation was a little awkward, because I preferred not to discuss the real reason for my visit on the telephone. However, having assured him that my purpose was not to ask for more money, I did in the end see him, did return half of the contribution, and did so, I believe, without in any way hurting his feelings.

134

Nine years later, I had a somewhat similar experience. In the course of my campaign for borough president of Manhattan, referred to in the previous chapter, Rockefeller had given me a modest contribution. In doing so, he had explained that he would have liked to have been more generous, but in view of the fact that the Democratic party dominated the governmental structure in New York City and in the light of the many delicate relationships existing between his real estate interests and City Hall, he hoped that I would understand his wish not to give anybody an excuse to discriminate against him unfairly. I did, of course, understand his position and was grateful for what he gave me.

After the conclusion of the campaign, in which, it will be recalled, I was overwhelmingly defeated, I was sitting one day writing thank you letters when the telephone rang and it was Nelson Rockefeller. "I have felt badly, Oren," he said, "that I gave you so small a contribution for your campaign. Now that the campaign is over, I would like tc help you with your deficit." Anybody who has had any experience with political campaigns knows how unusual and how generous this offer was, and I was quite overwhelmed by it. However, I found it necessary to report to him that my campaign had ended not with a deficit but with a tiny surplus, and could I have a rain check. Thus it was that my contacts with Nelson Rockefeller in the area of political contributions resulted in one case in my returning half his contribution and in another in declining it altogether.

I had a number of other contacts with Rockefeller during the decade of the forties, all of them giving clues to the generally liberal and progressive line along which his mind was developing at the time. He was, for example, one of the signers of the telegram which I organized, referred to in the preceding chapter, in support of a Federal Fair Employment Practices Act. He was one of the leaders whom I consulted when I was trying, at Governor Dewey's request, to put together a vehicle through which the Republican party in New York City might be revitalized. While I did not consult him with respect to Governor Dewey's suggestion that I run in the Republican primary against Congressman Joseph Clark Baldwin, in the course of a letter which Rockefeller wrote me in May of that year on another subject, he expressed passing regret that Baldwin, a noted liberal, was apparently being forced off the political scene.

One of the persons who encouraged this liberal and progressive bent in Rockefeller was Frank Jamieson. Jamieson, a former newspaperman and a person of broad acquaintance, friendly personality, and a background in Democratic politics, first joined Rockefeller in Washington when the latter was Coordinator of Inter-American Affairs during World War II under President Roosevelt. In later years he became senior public relations advisor to the Rockefeller family. Nelson Rockefeller had many advisors, reflecting many different political and social viewpoints. Of those advisors, it was Jamieson more than any other who helped Rockefeller, a lifelong Republican from an established Republican family, to hold to and develop his natural liberal and progressive instincts. It was also Jamieson who supported Rockefeller in his desire to include among his associates and acqaintances persons active in the labor movement, in the civil rights movement, and in other comparable areas not normally a part of the life of a young man of vast wealth.

It has been said that Ivy Lee moulded the image of the first John D. Rockefeller from that of a robber baron into that of a gentle philanthropist. If this be true, Frank Jamieson perhaps should be listed as Lee's latter-day counterpart, because of the role he played in helping to mould the conscience and the political tastes and proclivities of the most dynamic member of the third Rockefeller generation. Jamieson's death in 1960, shortly after Rockefeller entered upon his first term as governor was a great loss to all who knew him.

Active and successful as Rockefeller's life was in post-war New York City, public affairs continued to attract him. Accordingly, at the invitation of President Eisenhower, he returned to Washington in 1953 as undersecretary of Health, Education and Welfare. From that post he moved in 1954 to the White House as special assistant to the president, operating largely in the area of foreign affairs. While he threw himself into these activities with his usual energy and zest and while, especially in the work he did in setting up the structure of the Department of Health, Education and Welfare, he made significant contributions, he found life in appointive office increasingly frustrating. In the end, he came to the conclusion that the best way to be effective in the American political system was to have a power base of his own, which meant elective office. Accordingly, in 1955 he resigned his White House post and returned to New York to test the political waters. That was the year in which Averell Harriman entered upon his term as governor, which meant that the Republican nomination to run against Harriman at the end of that term was up for grabs.

III

Between the year 1955 and his nomination for governor in 1958, Rockefeller engaged in two very significant activities. He accepted the chairmanship of the Temporary State Commission on the Constitutional Convention, which was created by the Republican-controlled legislature to prepare for the constitutional convention which was scheduled for 1958 but which never took place because of an adverse popular

137

vote in the 1957 election. As counsel to that commission, Rockefeller retained George L. Hinman of Binghamton, New York, who was destined to play a major role in Rockefeller's future political life. Hinman is three years older than Rockefeller, a member of a distinguished upstate New York family, head of an old and successful Binghamton law firm, and a gentleman of infinite wisdom, patience, and human decency. His service to Rockefeller both in the state and in his three campaigns for the presidency has been skillful and devoted. Out of that service has come a close friendship, not only between the two men but also between Happy Rockefeller, the governor's warm and attractive second wife, and Hinman's beautiful and generous wife, Barbara. Also in the course of the work of that commission, Rockefeller developed an association with the brilliant and dynamic William Ronan, who later, as secretary to the governor, became Rockefeller's first chief of staff.

The other significant activity of those years was a series of reports relating to major public issues, both domestic and foreign, which were prepared and published by the Rockefeller Brothers Fund under the personal guidance and leadership of Nelson Rockefeller. Between these two activities, Rockefeller's name was very much in the headlines during the period in which the candidates for the Republican nomination for governor were under consideration.

In the early part of 1958 it became clear to me that Rockefeller was by far the best available candidate to run against Governor Harriman, who would almost certainly seek a second term. Not only did he have vast political and administrative experience in important government posts, as well as long-time identification with the Republican party, both individually and through his family, but he was ideologically in the great tradition of Theodore Roosevelt, Willkie, and Eisenhower, a tradition which had always found a warm response among voters of the Empire State. When I visited him to give him my views and express the hope that I could play a small role in advancing his candidacy, he was non-committal. However, I went away confident that his eye was on Albany and that he would achieve his goal. I also paid a number of visits to George Hinman on the same subject. My young sons and I were in the habit once or twice a year of visiting a beautiful Benedictine monastery in western New York, and it was convenient to stop on the way for a pleasant lunch with Hinman in Binghamton.

Rockefeller did, of course, have some hurdles to take. While he was well known at the national level and in civic and intellectual circles, he was a complete stranger to the large body of local Republican chieftains around the state whose views and actions would determine who the candidate would be. Politicians, even more than most other people, are fearful of unknown quantities. Was Rockefeller a real Republican or had he been contaminated by his service under two Democratic presidents? Would he be willing to deal fairly with the regular organization, or would he be so independent and high-handed that the organization would be left out in the cold? Attractive and energetic as he was, would he be prepared to undergo the grueling task of campaigning eighteen hours a day throughout the state's sixty-two counties? Did his long-time association with leaders of labor and leaders of the civil rights movement make him unsafe, as seen through the eyes of conservative businessmen from upstate cities and rural areas?

To help him answer these questions and take these hurdles, Rockefeller chose as guide, mentor, and friend one of the most experienced Republican figures in the state, Malcolm Wilson. Although only forty-four years old at the time, Malcolm Wilson had served as a Republican member of the legislature from Westchester County for twenty years. Preponderantly conservative in economic and social matters, but a stalwart advocate of individual liberties, deeply religious, and with the brilliant and precise intellect of a successful lawyer, Wilson provided everything that Rockefeller needed at the moment. Wilson's adherence to the legal process and his support of individual liberties were never better exemplified than by his testimony in later years as a character witness for two of his Democratic colleagues from the legislature who were being criminally prosecuted. Wilson had nothing in common with either of those men politically and little personally, but they asked him to testify to their public reputations and he concluded that it was his duty to do so, irrespective of the political risk involved.

During the spring and summer of 1958 Wilson and Rockefeller toured the state together in Wilson's automobile, calling on county chairmen and other political chieftains, all of whom Wilson knew on a first-name basis. There was no entourage and there were no advance men; there were neither agenda nor literature. There was just Malcolm Wilson with his friendships and with his character, and there was Nelson Rockefeller with his personality, his energy, his vast understanding of human nature and of world events, and his obvious desire to know and understand the people to whom he was being introduced. The response was electric, and Rockefeller's nomination for governor ensued with almost no significant dissent.

The campaign which followed was a model of élan and of efficiency. Gathered around the candidate were all the top people of his personal apparatus: Frank Jamieson, the brilliant public relations man; John Lockwood, the senior legal advisor to the Rockefeller family; Roswell Perkins, who had served as assistant secretary of HEW during Rockefeller's last period in Washington; and, in the background, the redoubtable Henry Kissinger, destined for great fame in later years, who for some time had been a foreign policy consultant to Rockefeller. Supplementing this talent were George Hinman, Malcolm Wilson, and Judson Morehouse, the attractive chairman of the Republican State Committee, who later unhappily came upon bad times, and a number of others. My own role was chairman of Citizens for Rockefeller-Keating, the Keating being Kenneth Keating, an outstandingly successful member of the House of Representatives, who had been persuaded by Rockefeller to run for United States Senator, and who later served on the New York Court of Appeals and then as President Nixon's ambassador to India and to Israel. The Citizens group, independently financed but closely coordinated with the main campaign effort, was designed to attract the independents and Democrats without whom no Republican can be elected governor in New York. It was the Willkie Clubs in microcosm, having much of the enthusiasm of the earlier groups, but lacking their spontaneity and independence.

Averell Harriman really never had a chance in that campaign. He had had a distinguished career as a foreign policy advisor to Presidents Roosevelt and Truman, including the embassy in Moscow, and was destined for further service in that area under Presidents Kennedy and Johnson. But the governorship was not his cup of tea. He was insecure in the political arena and apparently unhappy in the job. His awkward and ineffective campaign for reelection was totally overwhelmed by the whirlwind of the Rockefeller organization, enthusiasm, and energy. Not only did Rockefeller find support in the usual conservative Republican areas of the state, but he made deep inroads among independents and Democrats. Democrats for Rockefeller, with Roswell Gilpatrick as its chairman and Oscar Ruebhausen, Rockefeller's brilliant and high-minded fellow Dartmouth alumnus, as its moving force, was a significantly more effective organization than such committees usually are. Rockefeller himself was everywhere, holding rallies on the streets of Harlem, addressing Puerto Ricans in their native Spanish, and venturing generally into numberless nooks and crannies of voters where no Republican candidate had been seen for generations. When the ballots were counted on election night, Rockefeller had won by just short of three quarters of a million votes.

The victory was celebrated at an inaugural ball in a vast national guard armory in Albany, at which all the Republican leaders of the state joined with members of the large Rockefeller family and its entourage to dance to the strains of Cab Calloway's band. As the guests were leaving in the early morning hours, the men in dinner jackets and the ladies with their furs and their jewels, a light snow began to fall. Somebody was heard to remark that nothing like that evening had taken place since the Winter Palace in St. Petersburg.

IV

Rockefeller's election in 1970 to a fourth four-year term was a record-breaking event in modern New York history. Only Governor Clinton, the state's first governor, who was elected to seven three-year terms, has surpassed that accomplishment. Governor Smith was elected four times, but those were two-year terms. Governor Lehman was elected to four terms, but the first three of those terms were for two years; it was only Governor Lehman's last term which, by amendment to the New York Constitution, was for the new four-year period. So, except for Governor Clinton, the record is clearly Rockefeller's.

With the exception of the campaign in 1962 against

Robert Morgenthau, a high-minded gentleman but a stiff and an unimaginative candidate, all of Rockefeller's campaigns for reelection were uphill fights. A governor in office makes friends, but he also makes enemies, and party enrollment in New York State favors the Democrats by a proportion of three and a half to two. In both 1966 and 1970 Rockefeller's chances in the early days of those campaigns seemed in real doubt. This was especially true in 1970, when his opponent was the esteemed former associate justice of the Supreme Court, Arthur Goldberg. Never for a moment, however, did Rockefeller allow himself to be discouraged or to diminish his efforts. In both cases he came from behind to win by substantial margins.

There is no doubt that Rockefeller greatly enjoys being governor, and has enjoyed it more as the years have passed, especially during the period that his presidential ambitions no longer diverted his attention. He enjoys the problems of government; for him those problems are not irritations, but opportunities for testing his ingenuity and his leadership. He enjoys the give and take with the legislature, where his friendships and his influence are by no means limited to the Republican side of the aisle. Most of all, perhaps, he enjoys moving around the state and coming in direct contact with the people. He has traveled the state not only in the years in which he was running for reelection, and not only in the intermediate years in which he was supporting others, but even between elections as well. Thus, in most years of his governorship he has organized a series of what he calls "town meetings." These involve his spending half a day or a day in various localities of the state, where leaders of labor, industry, publishing, and other aspects of community life are gathered for a question-and-answer session with no holds barred. One of Rockefeller's greatest assets is his total mastery of facts and figures relating to matters under his jurisdiction. He can refer to them by memory with impressive exactness. As a consequence, there are few men who can handle themselves as effectively as he does in community gatherings of this kind.

Rockefeller runs the state, in the main, from two small adjoining reconstructed brownstone houses on West 55th Street, which he has owned for a number of years. When the legislature is in session, he takes up his residence in the Executive Mansion in Albany and he goes there from time to time in other seasons as the occasion demands. During most of the year, however, he operates from the small and modestly furnished room which serves as his office on the second floor of 22 West 55th Street.

There are those who have criticized Rockefeller for not spending enough time in Albany. There have even been times, especially during campaigns, when some people have tried to make it seem that his absence from Albany meant that he was inattentive to his duties. This is just plain silly. In the first place, a number of important government departments, including banking, insurance, and labor are run primarily from New York City. The Public Service Commission used also to be run from New York City, but recently the headquarters were moved to Albany by Joseph Swidler, the very able chairman of the commission whom Rockefeller brought from Washington to New York to reorganize it. In addition, getting to New York is a lot easier than getting to Albany for people from around the country, and in many instances even for people from other parts of New York State. In any case, with the telephone and other modern electronic communication devices and with his family airplane, the Rockefeller contacts between Albany and New York are such that he can operate with equal effectiveness from either place.

Rockefeller is an enormously hard worker. Not only does

he put in a full day at the office, but he invariably takes
home a briefcase bulging with reading matter. He is a morning person rather than a night person, with the consequence
that he tends to go to bed early and then, when he wakes up
very early the next morning, out comes the briefcase for a
couple of hours' work before breakfast. Some people operate
better by oral communication and others by written. Rockefeller operates well by both, but in view of the magnitude
of the demands upon his time, persons working with him
tend in ordinary circumstances to communicate by memorandum rather than by trying to see him. If the memorandum is sufficiently succinct and clear, it will be read
promptly and the writer will get it back with a few words of
gubernatorial comment scrawled across its face: "Thanks,
Oren," or "Good work, keep it up," or "I have some reservations—please see me about this," or some other similarly appropriate comment.

My first job with Rockefeller was as his special assistant
for federal and interstate relations. This required me to act
as his liaison with the members of Congress from New York
State, whom he had caused to be organized for that purpose
under the chairmanship of Congressman Emanuel Celler.
During this period Rockefeller was also active as a member
of the Governors Conference, which is an organization comprising all the governors in the country, which meets for
three or four days once a year and which functions in between such meetings through committees. During the period
that I was on his staff, Governor Rockefeller was chairman
of the Committee on Civil Defense. This was also the period
during which he developed his proposals for fall-out shelters,
designed to protect the population against atomic attack.
His work with the committee was therefore something he
took with great seriousness.

Going to a Governors Conference with Nelson Rockefeller

145

was an experience not to be forgotten. For many governors the annual gathering is a kind of semi-vacation. The host state customarily pays the expenses for each governor and a limited number of other persons. The governors have to pay their own traveling expenses, but in many cases travel is arranged in national guard planes. This is important, since a number of governors fill at least some of their quota with members of their families, whose traveling expenses could not properly be charged to their official travel accounts if they traveled commercially.

With Rockefeller, however, a Governors Conference was quite another story. He was always accompanied by ten or twelve staff persons, all without wives and all of whose expenses were paid by Rockefeller personally. While other governors might be taking sight-seeing tours, or enjoying the outdoor recreational facilities, Rockefeller's staff, which probably started the day by meeting with him at breakfast, would carry through, with only the briefest interludes for rest, into the early hours of the next morning. Not only did Rockefeller himself always have a series of resolutions which required drafting and research, but he frequently made his staff available to other governors who were supporting resolutions with which he was sympathetic and who lacked adequate staffs of their own.

It was out of my work as liaison with the Committee on Civil Defense that there came one of the very few difficult experiences I had with Rockefeller. He had asked me to draft a memorandum on a matter relating to the work of that committee and to have it on his desk in his 55th Street office by the end of the day. Since I knew that Dr. Ronan, his chief of staff, was immersed in some aspects of the problem which was to be the subject of my memorandum, I went to consult him. He told me that he was preparing for the governor a memorandum on a related subject and suggested that he include in his memorandum the items which the governor had directed me to cover in mine. I agreed, and, having left the matter in such competent hands, proceeded to forget it.

As it turned out, that was a great mistake. In those days I used to commute from New York City to northern Westchester by train. As I arrived home that evening about seven o'clock, my wife told me that Rockefeller had called and had left a number at which I was to telephone him as soon as I came in. She added that the governor had not sounded very happy, that she had tried to chat a little with him, but that he was all business. When I got him on the telephone at the number which he had left, he asked for the memorandum which he had commissioned that morning. I told him what had transpired with Dr. Ronan, to which he replied, "When I ask you for a memorandum, Oren, I want to get it from you. I would appreciate it if you would have that memorandum on my desk at nine o'clock tomorrow morning."

Naturally, I was contrite, especially since I knew the governor was right and that I had not done what he had asked me to do. However, there I was forty-five miles from New York at seven o'clock in the evening with no typing facilities. What made the matter even worse was that I could not prepare the memorandum alone but needed some help from sources which were in New York and not in northern Westchester, especially from Oscar Ruebhausen, who was one of Rockefeller's leading experts on matters relating to atomic energy in general and fall-out shelters in particular. There then happened one of those happy episodes which enrich human life. I telephoned Ruebhausen at his apartment in New York and told him of my predicament. His reply was that he had an entirely free evening and that if I could be at his apartment by 9:30 he would be glad to help me with the memorandum. He not only did this, but his attractive

147

wife, Zelia, sat up with us until well after midnight typing
it. The memorandum was on the governor's desk before nine
the next morning and I was both wiser with respect to my
relationship with him and deeply in debt to the Ruebhausens
for their coming to my rescue with such warmth and friendship.

At the end of 1960, I left Rockefeller's staff and returned
to my law firm. In late spring of the following year, I sought
an appointment with him on a personal matter. He has
always been very generous in seeing me when I asked, and
I received an appointment promptly. Before I had a chance
even to discuss what was on my mind, however, he took me
completely by surprise by offering me the post of superintendent of banks, from which position he told me his then
appointee, Russell Clark, was about to resign. Since I knew
very little about the functions of that office and since, in
addition, I felt I should consult with my partners and with
my family, I asked whether I could have some time to think
it over. He told me yes, that I could have some time, but
that he hoped the response would come fairly quickly because Clark was pressing to vacate the office. He then made
an interesting and characteristic comment: "Most of the
things which I have done in my life from which I have de-
rived satisfaction I did spontaneously. I hope you will benefit from my experience." A few days later I accepted his
offer and a few days after that I was sworn in. I never regretted the decision. Working for him in this new capacity
was quite different from working on his staff, however, because I was administering a department of several hundred
persons and I had statutory responsibilities in my own right,
apart from the powers and responsibilities that I held de-
rivatively as his appointee.

The principal issues during my term in the Banking Department revolved around the branching and merging of

banks and the formation of bank holding companies. It has long been a cardinal principle in the United States, and New York State has been no exception, that the welfare of the public was best served by a broad dispersal of banking power, so that individuals requiring banking services would always have a large number of institutions between which to choose. Accordingly, the laws of New York and other jurisdictions were designed in large part to protect the integrity of small banks and to restrict the expansion, by branching and merging, of large ones. But with the developing complexities of modern banking it became increasingly clear that small unit banks were no longer equal to the demands of the times and that some relaxation of the statutory restrictions was in order. The result was a series of amendments to the New York Banking Law enacted by the legislature in 1960 and 1961 with Governor Rockefeller's support, which took steps in that direction.

Following those amendments there was a major spurt in applications for new bank branches, for mergers between banks, and for the formation of bank holding companies. It was my view that the public interest would best be served by the approval of as many of those applications as did not violate the still very strict mandates of the statutes, and I acted accordingly. Indeed, I sponsored a bill in the legislature which would have expanded still further the areas in which banks could branch and merge. While my bill passed the Assembly, it failed in the Senate, where the opposition of the smaller upstate banks was more influential. Ultimately, under one of my successors, an even more liberal bill was adopted and is the law of the state today.

As superintendent of banks I always had the governor's full support. Never in the three years that I was in that office did he seek to influence or direct my course of action in the discharge of my statutory duties, although I have no

149

doubt, because of the magnitude of the stakes involved, that there were times when he was importuned to do so. On the other hand, while I did not often need to seek his help or advice, when I did seek them they were always forthcoming. He was an ideal boss and my service in that post was an altogether satisfactory experience.

While Rockefeller expected his staff and his cabinet to work as hard as he did, he was always considerate of their welfare and their comfort. In traveling with him, his associates usually shared his private plane and the hotel accommodations provided for them were invariably good and comfortable. From time to time he was the host at social events, sometimes at his apartment in New York, sometimes at his princely estate in Pocantico Hills, and sometimes in the Executive Mansion in Albany. Whether these events were official or personal, appropriate members of his staff and his cabinet were almost always included. If the event took place in the evening and circumstances required him to do so, as, for example, when a distinguished dinner dance was given in the Executive Mansion for the Crown Princess of the Netherlands, he would stay up until whatever hour the guest of honor chose to remain. In other and more intimate gatherings, however, he felt free to indulge his normal habit of reasonably early retirement.

One occasion which my wife and I attended and which fell into the latter category took place on New Year's Eve, just prior to the beginning of his second term. It was a dinner for about forty persons at the mansion, most of whom were members of his family and close associates from the staff and the cabinet. Included in the guest list were former attorney general of the United States Herbert Brownell and his wife, who, because of a business engagement in Washington that day, had had a very long trip and did not arrive until shortly after the other guests had been seated. After dinner all the guests repaired to the drawing room and settled themselves down looking forward to the stroke of midnight, at which time they anticipated a glass of champagne, a toast to the New Year, and to the new gubernatorial term. It had been a long day for the governor, however, and at 10:30 he said good night and went to bed. The rest of us looked at each other and then decided to take the hint and depart. Many of the guests lived in the Albany area. Leaving before midnight did not matter to them, since they went home to their private celebrations. For the Brownells and my wife and me, however, having no home to go to in the Albany area, the situation was different. Accordingly, we repaired to the bar of the DeWitt Clinton Hotel, where we drank the New Year in with steins of beer. It was a New Year's Eve we will not quickly forget.

Since Rockefeller is still in office and may have a fifth term, it is too early to assess definitively his talents and his accomplishments. By way of interim assessment, however, it seems safe to say that he has been an outstanding governor. His record in public housing, in transportation, in massive efforts to clean the air and the waters, have made a mark from which the public will long benefit. An additional accomplishment, in some ways perhaps his most outstanding one, has been the development of the State University of New York, on the board of which I sit by his appointment. The university, which had 38,000 full-time students when he first came to office in 1959, had by 1973 grown to 235,000 full-time students, and this growth was accomplished while giving generous government support to the hard pressed private universities and colleges as well.

Probably the greatest single criticism of Rockefeller's record in office relates to the fiscal consequences of his programs. There is no doubt that during his term as governor the state of New York and the various independent and

151

semi-independent agencies which operate at the state level have borrowed a very large sum of money and have spent a great deal as well. The state budget has increased from under two billion dollars in 1959 to almost nine billion for fiscal year 1974, without counting the budgets of various independent agencies and authorities. Taxes have risen sharply. A large part of this, however, must be attributed to inflation, over which a governor has no control. Moreover, a major part of the moneys collected at the state level are returned to the municipalities and other local governments to help finance education and other services at those levels.

New York State has been unusually fortunate in its modern governors. Without exception, they have been decent, intelligent, public-spirited men, and in some cases they have been outstanding. In addition, the state has been the beneficiary of a succession of men in the position of counsel to the governor, who, although frequently unheralded and unsung, have played major roles in promoting the public welfare. Among such men have been Charles Breitel, Lawrence Walsh, and George Shapiro in the Dewey administrations and Roswell Perkins, Robert MacCrate, Sol Corbin, Robert Douglass, and Michael Whiteman under Rockefeller. These are the men who, under the guidance and direction of their respective governors and with the cooperation of the legislative leaders, have protected the public from an overwhelming mass of ill-considered legislative proposals. Through his counsel's office a governor exercises considerable influence over pending legislation even while it is still at the legislative level, and it is to that office that a governor primarily looks for advice in deciding which bills to sign and which to veto. The importance of this role can be understood when it is remembered that in the legislative session of 1972 over 18,000 bills were introduced (including carry-overs from the previous session), of which slightly less than 1,300 passed both houses, and of those only a little over a thousand were ultimately signed into law.

V

There appears to be a real possibility that Rockefeller will make a fourth attempt at the presidency in 1976. President Nixon is constitutionally barred from a third term, and if Rockefeller is elected in 1974 to a fifth term as governor, a new try for the White House certainly cannot be ruled out. On the other hand, there are significant obstacles in his way, the most important of which is his age. Rockefeller will be sixty-eight years old in 1976 and, if nominated, would be the oldest presidential candidate in modern times. It may be that his natural vigor will overcome that handicap, however, and that circumstances will cause the party and the country to turn to him for leadership.

In spite of all his vast accomplishments in the state of New York and in the philanthropic and other theaters in which he has operated through his private fortune, Rockefeller's failure thus far to achieve the presidency has thrown a shadow of incompleteness over his life. His worldwide vision, his magnificent sense of organization, his natural proclivity for the management of great affairs—these, more even than his ambition, have been frustrated by his not having achieved the summit. It is nevertheless much to his credit that, while obviously disappointed, he has attained an inner security which has enabled him to rise above this frustration. Perhaps he takes comfort in the historic fact that the men who reach the presidency are not always the greatest men of their times. He can thus console himself that his failure, thus far at least, in this respect puts him in the company of such great men as Henry Clay, Daniel Webster,

John W. Davis, Al Smith, and Wendell Willkie, all of whom were giants in their day and all of whom tried for the ultimate prize and missed it.

Anyone viewing Rockefeller's prospects for the presidency at the end of 1958 would have had to say they were outstanding. His strong victory at the polls that year placed him on a springboard which historically had led to the White House. In the early years of the Republic it was Virginia which was the mother of presidents, but in modern times it has been New York, if not of presidents at least of presidential candidates. In the twenty-three presidential campaigns from 1868 to 1956, there were fifteen elections in which one or the other or both of the major candidates came from New York, not counting John W. Davis and Wendell Willkie, who, although living in New York at the time of their nominations, had no significant political base in that state. Of these New York candidates, all but two had been governors of the state.

In addition, Rockefeller certainly wanted to be president. His early government experiences were in Washington, and he never gave up the house which he occupied during the time in which he lived there. His thinking and his attitudes have always been essentially national and global. In this connection, I recall something he said to me shortly after his first election and before he took office in Albany. We were sitting together in one of the lounges of the University Club on Fifth Avenue, by coincidence only a small distance from where I had sat with Willkie eighteen years earlier on the morning that he consented that I continue with my campaign on behalf of his nomination. As we sat together, Rockefeller told me of his plans to establish a New York State office in Washington, and we discussed the kind of liaison with the Congressional delegation which was ultimately to be one of my duties as his special assistant for federal and interstate relations. And then he made a very revealing comment. "The country is in real danger, Oren," he said, "confronted with vast perils both foreign and domestic. We do not have much time. We can, of course, do many worthwhile things here in New York, but the great issues will be decided in Washington. That is why I want to have an office there and that is why I want you to have a role in it." Although the office never became the important factor he envisaged that night, his comment in referring to it was interesting.

Why have Rockefeller's quests for the presidency been unsuccessful? Given his outstanding talents, his vast resources, and the springboard of the governorship of New York, why has he failed not only to become president, but why in three gallant tries has he failed even to gain the nomination? He has failed, in my opinion, partly because he wanted the office too much and partly because he did not want it badly enough.

In 1959, in the early period of his Albany tenure, many of Rockefeller's advisors were of the view that the best thing for him to do about the presidency was to ignore it. In the first place, they knew that being governor of New York, dealing with the legislature and establishing a reputation as a viable administrator, was not something to be done part-time. Beyond that, they were of the view that the best method for Rockefeller to attract the presidential nomination was to do so outstanding a job in the governorship, in the full glare of the publicity with which that office is inevitably surrounded, that the party would beat a path to his door.

But Rockefeller thought otherwise. The course advocated by his advisors might cause the party leaders to come to him in the end, but would they come in 1960? And if they did not, and if Richard Nixon, the most likely nominee, won the White House in 1960, would that not close the door to

Rockefeller for eight long years? And who could foretell the future anyway? Midway through his first year in office, Rockefeller saw himself with his luck running at full tide, fresh from a notable electoral victory in the Empire State and with one successful legislative session behind him. Why, then, take the risks of unexpected adverse turns of fate? In other words, why wait?

And so in the early fall of 1959 the decision was made to test the national waters. It was not that Rockefeller underestimated the job of being governor, or his duties to New York, because he is a very conscientious man. It was because, being Nelson Rockefeller, nothing seemed impossible, and he saw no reason why he could not fully discharge his duties as governor and run for president at the same time. So the campaign staff of the year before was reactivated, with a few changes and some additions. Included in the latter category were R. Burdell Bixby, a close associate of Governor Dewey's, and Emmet John Hughes, an able writer who had served with President Eisenhower and who in the period of Rockefeller's presidential efforts developed with him a very close rapport.

The presidential probe was carried on throughout the fall of 1959. Political emissaries fanned out from Rockefeller headquarters on West 55th Street to talk with state chairmen and others around the country who might command delegates. Emissaries of the Rockefeller family, with its multi-faceted resources, moved out to inquire about help and support from the sources with which they had long been in association. Rockefeller himself made a number of speaking tours, hoping to arouse the kind of popular response which had successfully pressured the delegates at the convention in 1940. But everywhere the doors were closed. The careful work which had been done by Nixon and his associates during the preceding two years had paid off. The persons controlling the Republican party at the time were satisfied that Nixon could win in 1960 and were convinced that Nixon was their kind of candidate. So why take a chance with a new face? Why rock the boat?

Thus it was, having learned from his probe that he could not take the party by storm, and faced as he was with the necessity of mounting an exhausting series of fights in primaries for which he was ill prepared, during a period when he would also have to deal with his second legislative session in Albany, that Rockefeller in the closing days of 1959 publicly withdrew from the race.

As it turned out, however, Rockefeller's withdrawal was not final. President Eisenhower had planned a summit meeting the following spring with Khrushchev, the Soviet leader. Just prior to that meeting, in early May, there occurred the famous U-2 incident, whereby it became public knowledge that the United States, contrary to its public statements, was surveying the Soviet Union by means of a high altitude photographic airplane. Khrushchev either felt or feigned deep shock. In any event, the proposed summit meeting collapsed and the prestige of the United States and its president were severely injured, at least in the short run. Ever since his days in the White House, Rockefeller had had reservations about the Eisenhower foreign policy. During the winter and spring of 1960 these reservations had strengthened and deepened. The collapse of the summit was only the most dramatic of the events which, taken together, propelled him into action.

Accordingly, in the late spring of 1960 Rockefeller returned to the political fray, first with a series of broad and sweeping public statements which were clearly critical of the national administration of which Nixon was a part, and then later by at least tacit acknowledgement of his candidacy for the nomination. There seemed at that point of time, at least to Rockefeller and his advisors (among whom at that moment Emmet Hughes played a leading role), to be a chance that the fateful turn of world events would bring him a favorable wind at the convention after all. However, his late spring effort was as unsuccessful as far as the nomination was concerned as the earlier one had been. On the other hand, by his famous and dramatic Fifth Avenue Compact with Nixon, Rockefeller did have a significant and constructive effect upon the party platform.

There are some persons who believe that Rockefeller's mistake in 1959–60 was his December withdrawal, that Nixon was more vulnerable than he appeared, and that had Rockefeller persisted through the primaries he would have prevailed. It is probable that this is what Rockefeller himself believes. However, there are others who believe that it was the prematureness of the early probe which undermined what could have been the effectiveness of the later effort. These people are of the view that if Rockefeller had bided his time, that if he had stayed in Albany during the fall and winter of 1959–60, demonstrating there his mastery of the arts of government and of the delicate political niceties, the events which transpired during the spring of 1960 on the world stage might indeed have caused the party to beat a path to his door, as world events had influenced the Willkie convention twenty years before. Nobody, of course, can prove the matter one way or the other. However, if the viewpoint just expressed is correct, then Rockefeller was truly denied the nomination for the reason that he wanted it too much. Indeed, there are some who would say that the prematureness of the early probe cost him the presidency itself, those persons being of the opinion that had he been the nominee instead of Nixon, the very close November victory of John F. Kennedy would have gone the other way.

It was four years later that Rockefeller lost the presidency because he did not want it badly enough. After his failure to take the party by storm in 1960, he and his advisors set upon a different course. This time they would organize in advance, state by state, delegation by delegation, and this time they would go into the primaries, at least in a few critical states. Having won reelection in New York in 1962 by a margin of over half a million votes, his electoral power in his home base was firmly established. The fact that this victory followed by about a year the announcement of his proposed divorce from his first wife made it all the more impressive. But his vote-getting power needed to be proved in other areas of the country and Rockefeller was prepared this time to prove it.

Starting immediately after the 1962 gubernatorial victory, the organizing began. Under the leadership of George Hinman, with help from others, the effort to gain support around the country went forward. The response was encouraging almost beyond hopes. The story everywhere was the exact opposite of 1959 and 1960. In the first place, the alternative to Rockefeller this time was not Nixon but Senator Barry Goldwater, who was also organizing actively in areas of the party sympathetic to his views; and to large numbers of responsible Republicans the prospect of a Goldwater nomination was appalling. In the second place, Rockefeller, instead of trying to appeal over the heads of the party machinery, as he had in his 1959–60 efforts, was, through Hinman, assiduously cultivating that machinery. By the spring of 1963, six months after the effort began, the reports coming in were overwhelmingly favorable. Equally important, the polls showed Rockefeller was the leading choice of Republican rank and file voters.

Then came the announcement that Rockefeller and Happy Murphy had married. Some few of Rockefeller's closest advisors had known of his intentions to remarry for some time. Without exception they had advised him that if he married again he would be gravely risking his chances for the nomination, which at that time seemed so very good. Whether or not such a step in a man's personal life should affect his political prospects is beside the point. His advisors knew that in the world in which we live it would affect them and would affect them adversely, as indeed it did.

Rockefeller weighed that advice and decided against it. It was not that he disagreed as to the risk; as a shrewd analyst of public opinion, he understood the risk at least as well as his advisors. It was partly the old Rockefeller conviction that everything is possible and that, granting the risk, he could nevertheless overcome it. But mainly it was that if he had to choose between the presidency and his marriage, he would choose the marriage. That marriage has been a fulfilling one and I have no doubt at all that if he had the decision to make over today he would follow the same course.

After the announcement the campaign faltered badly, but it continued. The effort to commit delegates in states without primaries went on under Hinman's skillful guidance, and vast preparations were made for the major primaries. By the spring of 1964 some of the momentum had been regained, but by no means all, and, as matters turned out, not enough.

Rockefeller lost in New Hampshire but won brilliantly in Oregon. Then he was nosed out by Goldwater in a bitter and probably critical primary in California, just a few weeks before the convention. Had he won in California, the convention result would almost certainly have been different. His record then from New Hampshire to California would have been an ascending one. And the result in California was so very close—Goldwater won by less than fifty-two percent—that clearly but for the adverse political effect of his remarriage Rockefeller would have prevailed. He wanted the presidency greatly, but there were other things in life he wanted more, and he made his choice. As a consequence, Goldwater was nominated and Lyndon Johnson swept the election the following November in the greatest victory since Franklin Roosevelt defeated Landon in 1936.

Rockefeller's third try for the presidency came in 1968. After his enormous exertions in 1964, he recoiled from another effort. For many months during the year leading up to the convention he gave his total support—political, personal and financial—to George Romney. Romney was the attractive, vigorous, and liberal governor of Michigan, and Rockefeller was of the view that he was the best qualified person to carry the banner of moderate Republicans.

In spite of Rockefeller's strenuous support, Romney proved unable to transfer to the national level the success he had had in Michigan. His famous statement about having been "brainwashed" in connection with a visit to Vietnam hurt him badly. The Romney candidacy never got off the ground. Accordingly, Rockefeller in the end announced that he would be a candidate for the nomination after all. As in 1960, it was too late for the primaries. Thus, as in 1960 Rockefeller set out to storm the convention by appealing to the voters over the heads of the party apparatus. The assassination of Robert Kennedy early in June gave his efforts an added impulse. Rockefeller would now appeal not only to the Republicans, not only to those of no party, but even to the Democrats who had followed Kennedy and were disaffected with President Johnson. He would appeal, as Kennedy had, to the poor, to the forgotten, and to the blacks, with whom by virtue of generations of Rockefeller philanthropy as well as by personal inclination he had a special rapport. By these appeals he would prove his transcendent political power, which hopefully would be reflected in the polls, and thus overwhelm the convention as Willkie had done in 1940.

It was a gallant try and it might have worked, but it did not. Richard Nixon was nominated in Miami and went on to win the election. For Nelson Rockefeller it was, barring only some future dramatic and unexpected turn of events, the end of a long quest. Just past sixty years old at that time, it seemed improbable that he could or would make another try for the presidency. He nevertheless did not permit this fact to embitter him. On the contrary, he returned with greater zest than ever to his duties as governor, as a result of which he has achieved a position of dominance in the politics of New York State unequalled in modern times. If there is any safe prophecy in this uncertain world, it is that, whether or not he makes a final try for the White House in 1976 and irrespective of the result of that try if he makes it, Nelson Rockefeller will one way or another continue as a constructive force as long as he lives. So far as the presidency is concerned, strong men have historically had a better chance for that office in periods of crisis or turmoil than in periods of tranquillity. It could be, therefore, that 1976 will, after all, be Nelson Rockefeller's year.

VI

The background of Jacob K. Javits is as different from Nelson Rockefeller's as one can possibly imagine. He was born and grew up on the lower east side of New York City, the son of a Jewish immigrant who worked as a janitor for three large tenements at a salary of $45 a month plus rooms. By hard work, and with the help of his devoted brother, Benjamin, who was ten years older and in some ways more a father than a brother, Javits received his education and was admitted to the New York Bar in 1927.

It would be natural to expect a person of Javits's background to be a Democrat. That he did not become a Democrat was due in large part, he has said, to the opportunity which he had to see at close hand the evils of the Tammany-run Democratic machine in New York City. It was also due, no doubt, to the appearance upon the political scene at a critical moment in Javits's life of Fiorello La Guardia. Javits supported La Guardia in his campaigns for mayor, and then, following the war, played a role in the mayoralty campaign of Judge Jonah Goldstein, the Republican-Fusion candidate who in 1945 ran for mayor and was defeated by William O'Dwyer.

Partly as a result of the work which Javits did in the Goldstein campaign, he was offered in 1946 the Republican nomination for Congress in the twenty-first Congressional District of Manhattan on the upper west side. It was not the most attractive of opportunities. Registration favored the Democrats by a two to one majority, and no Republican had been elected to Congress from the area for twenty-three years. However, by virtue of friendships which he had developed with Alex Rose and David Dubinsky during the Goldstein campaign, Javits received the nomination of the Liberal party as well. He organized an intelligent and unusually energetic campaign which, to the surprise of many, was successful. He was reelected in 1948, 1950, and 1952. In the 1952 voting he won by the extraordinary margin of two to one, carrying the district on the Republican line alone.

In 1954 Javits was elected attorney general of New York in a great personal triumph, beating Franklin D. Roosevelt, Jr., by better than 172,000 votes while Senator Ives, the head of the ticket, was losing the governorship by a narrow margin. Two years later, he was elected to the United States Senate in the Eisenhower landslide of 1956, defeating Robert F. Wagner, Jr., then mayor of New York. He was reelected to the Senate in 1962 and again in 1968, very considerable accomplishments in the face of the preponderance of Democratic enrollment in the state.

I had the opportunity to participate, to a greater or lesser degree, in all of Javits's campaigns. They were always tightly knit, well organized, and extremely energetic. Virtually all the money to finance the campaigns was raised by Javits personally, with the help of his brother, Ben, and of a small circle of close associates. The relationship between the two brothers was an intimate one of great mutual respect and loyalty. In 1947 Javits married his beautiful and stimulating wife, Marion, who thereafter became a significant influence upon his life.

Partly because of his independent nature, Javits has never become a member of the inner circle in the United States Senate, with the result that his influence in that body has sometimes been less than his intellect, his energy, and his coming from New York State would seem to indicate. In addition, while he has achieved a high degree of visibility and public recognition, he has not developed the kind of father figure image which was developed by Herbert Lehman in his time. Nevertheless, with the help of the large and brilliant staff he has assembled, he has sponsored huge quantities of legislation in Washington, much of which has become law, and he has played a role of significant leadership in the North Atlantic Treaty Organization and on the Foreign Relations Committee and other committees of the Senate.

There are some, particularly among members of his own party, who have criticized Javits for being too liberal. It is true that on social matters and matters relating to individual liberties he has been avowedly liberal. However, in fiscal matters and in matters affecting the vitality of the free enterprise system he has been surprisingly conservative. Also, while he has necessarily built up his large electoral majorities with appeals to Democrats and independents as well as to Republicans, he has always gone out of his way to maintain correct and, in some instances, even close relationships with the Republican leaders of the state. There has been some natural and inevitable rivalry at times between Rockefeller and Javits, but Javits has made it his business to see that this rivalry was kept within bounds. Fundamentally, there is considerable mutual respect between the two men. Indeed, Rockefeller's support of Javits dates back to the early days of Javits's career, long before Rockefeller ran for governor. This is as it should be, because one of Javits's most significant contributions to his times lies in the fact of his being a Republican. The diversity and originality which he has brought to the Republican party constitute a major contribution to the two-party system.

My personal relations with Javits have always been warm and friendly, and my wife and his wife have had much in common. One of my prized possessions is a wrist watch given me after his first campaign for the United States Senate inscribed on the back "for devoted service—Marion, Ben & Jack Javits."

VII

John V. Lindsay at the beginning of his political career appeared the prototype of the successful public servant. Scion of a modestly wealthy family, a graduate of St. Paul's School, one of the most exclusive of the eastern preparatory schools, and of Yale, married to the attractive daughter of an established Connecticut family, he seemed very much in the tradition of the Lodges and the Saltonstalls in Massachusetts. But his career was destined for more turbulence than that.

Lindsay's first contact with politics came in 1940 when he and his twin brother were pages on the floor of the 1940 convention in Philadelphia where Wendell Willkie was nominated. Undoubtedly, that experience had a strong influence on his thinking and attitudes, as it did upon the thinking and attitudes of so many others. Perhaps it had something to do with the fact that when I ran for the office of borough president of Manhattan nine years later, John and Mary Lindsay were among my supporters and arranged a gathering of their friends for me in their small apartment.

In its early stages Lindsay's political career was almost too successful to be true. After a two-year period as executive assistant to the attorney general of the United States, Herbert Brownell, he won election to Congress from what was then the Seventeenth District of New York, known because it comprised among its voters so many rich and powerful people, as the silk stocking district. That seat had been occupied for six terms by Frederic R. Coudert, an intelligent but exceedingly conservative lawyer. Partly because of changes in the character of the district, with the kind of voters who tended to be Republican moving increasingly to the suburbs, and partly because in his later years he was not as energetic in the pursuit of his public duties as he had been in the earlier period, Coudert's hold upon the district was showing signs of weakening, and he decided not to run for reelection in 1958. Accordingly, Lindsay ran for the nomination in the Republican primary that year and won. He then went on to win the election. Altogether Lindsay served four terms in Congress, always winning by substantial majorities and always running ahead of his ticket. Because of the quality of his victories, the location of his district, and the vigor with which he addressed himself to his job, both in Washington and among his constituents, Lindsay at the time was one of the best known younger members of the House of Representatives.

In 1965 Lindsay was elected mayor of New York City in a

dramatic political upset. He had the nomination of both the Republican party and the Liberal party, but the voter enrollment in the city was over three to one Democratic, and no Republican had been elected mayor since La Guardia. By a strange twist of fate, his victory may have been brought about in the closing days of the campaign by the assaults upon him by William F. Buckley, the articulate political columnist and commentator, who ran as the candidate of the Conservative party. Buckley knew he had no chance to win and his principal purpose in running (apart from the joy of the fray, in which he reveled) was to help insure a Lindsay defeat. However, his attacks on Lindsay were so virulent that he roused a section of the electorate which, while not friendly to Lindsay, was deeply fearful of what they regarded as Buckley's excessively conservative views. Accordingly, those people voted for Lindsay not so much because they liked him as because they did not want Buckley to have the credit for his defeat. In 1969 Lindsay lost the Republican nomination in the primary but went on to win reelection on the Liberal line alone. This considerable personal victory was brought about in part, however, by his having an especially ineffective Democratic opponent.

The life of a mayor of New York is turbulent by definition, but John Lindsay's has been especially so. He began his first term with the necessity of facing a transit strike under the leadership of the colorful leprechaun Michael Quill, leader of the Transit Workers Union. Where Robert Wagner, Lindsay's predecessor as mayor, had developed friendly contacts with the strong men in the city's labor movement, Lindsay denounced those same men, by implication at least, as "power brokers." Thus where Wagner had been able to enlist labor support in negotiating wage settlements behind the scenes, Lindsay was faced with open and public confrontations.

It was not long before there developed for John Lindsay another confrontation, this time with Governor Rockefeller. The city of New York is dependent to a much larger degree than most people realize upon Albany. Its taxing powers are given it by the legislature in Albany, and the limits of its borrowing powers are determined there as well. In addition, a very large part of its funds come not from its own taxing power but by the distribution to it of state moneys which, although raised in part from New York City taxpayers, are controlled by and disbursed from Albany. Moreover, the state of New York has the power to investigate, privately or publicly, any aspect of city government, and over the years, including recent years, it has used this power freely. The governor has the power, subject only to certain reasonably simple precedures, to remove any city official from office, including the mayor. Indeed, Mayor Walker's resignation in 1932 came about because it was widely believed that had he not resigned Governor Roosevelt would have removed him.

Because of the state-city relationship described above, there is a natural antagonism between mayors of the city and governors of the state. Mayors through the years have contended that the city does not get its fair share of the tax dollars collected and distributed by the state, and they have amassed a series of statistics to prove that point. Governors, on the other hand, have always contended that the trouble with the city is that it does not know how to spend efficiently the very large sums which the state disburses to it, and the governors have been able to show that state aid to the city has grown both steadily and dramatically.

In the case of Rockefeller and Lindsay, the tensions inherent in their positions were magnified by their temperaments. Both are able men; both are proud men. Partly because of his greater age, partly because of the seniority of his office, and partly because he has sincerely believed that

168

he had a better concept of what is good for New York City than Lindsay, Rockefeller expected a certain deference from the mayor. But Lindsay was not one to defer, and so they clashed. Most of the time the surface amenities were maintained, because both men are disciplined gentlemen. Sometimes even those surface amenities have been strained, however, as in the unfortunate strike of garbage collectors during Lindsay's first term in City Hall. In that strike the mayor wanted the governor to call out the National Guard, which only the governor had the power to do. Instead, Rockefeller negotiated a settlement of the strike, which was then forced upon an unwilling and unhappy Lindsay. This was probably the low point of their personal relationship.

In addition to the frustrations inherent in city government and in the difficulties arising out of his less than happy relationship with Rockefeller, Lindsay became increasingly troubled by his membership in the Republican party. In an episode which he no doubt now regrets, Lindsay made an unsuccessful effort to win the Republican nomination for vice president in Miami in 1968, and ended up by making one of the seconding speeches for Spiro Agnew. Ideologically, however, he found himself drifting further and further from the positions held by leading Republicans, especially on the issue of the Vietnam War. More importantly, perhaps, with a Republican governor and one Republican and one Conservative senator in New York, and with a Republican president in Washington, all doors to his electoral advancement in that party seemed to be closed. It was thus that in the spring of 1972 Lindsay switched to the Democratic party. Whether he will be any happier there and whether, in the light of his decision not to seek a third term as mayor, he can keep his political prospects for other office alive, only time will tell.

I do not know whether or not it is true, as was rumored at

169

the time, that Rockefeller was prepared in 1968 to appoint Lindsay to the United States Senate to fill the vacancy caused by Robert Kennedy's death, but, fearful that Lindsay might rebuff the appointment, insisted that Lindsay ask for it if he wanted it. If that story is true, Lindsay should have asked for it, because, with his conceptual orientation and his capacity for articulate expression, he would have been happier there and probably more effective than he has been in City Hall.

VIII

Since Franklin D. Roosevelt and Herbert Lehman, the Democratic party has developed no outstanding personality in New York State. Averell Harriman had a distinguished career in appointive office at the federal level under four presidents, but he was unhappy and ineffective in Albany. Various Democratic mayors of New York City—O'Dwyer, Impellitteri, Wagner—were never successful in expanding beyond the limits of the metropolis. Franklin Roosevelt, Jr., the attractive and talented son of a distinguished father, started to climb the political ladder at the state level by running for attorney general on the ticket with Averell Harriman in 1954. It was Roosevelt's misfortune to come up against Jacob Javits in that race, and Javits beat him, even though Harriman carried the top of the ticket. In 1966 the Liberal party gave Roosevelt its nomination for governor, hoping that he would repeat his dramatic independent victory for Congress of seven years earlier. But the circumstances were different and his political glamor was not what it had been prior to his defeat by Javits. He got only slightly in excess of half a million votes. However, his independent candidacy, by dividing the Democratic-Liberal vote, was helpful to Governor Rockefeller in achieving reelection.

The one exception to the general level of mediocrity in the Democratic party in New York State could have been Robert Kennedy, who moved there from Massachusetts and was elected to the Senate in 1964. But that possibility was ended by his assassination, and no Democrat since then has moved into the vacuum caused by his death. Lindsay may still try to do so, and so may Ogden Reid of Westchester County. Reid is a descendent of one of the founders of the Republican party, a grandson of a Republican ambassador to the Court of St. James's, and himself one of the last publishers of the leading Republican newspaper of that time, the *Herald Tribune.*

Having returned from a tour as Eisenhower's ambassador to Israel, Reid served five terms as a Republican member of the House of Representatives. Like John Lindsay, however, he found it increasingly difficult to adjust his ideology to the prevailing thinking of the Republican party and, like John Lindsay, he saw all doors to his political advancement in that party barred to him. Accordingly, a few months after Lindsay became a Democrat, Reid did the same thing. In Reid's case he had to run for reelection in the fall of 1972, campaigning for the first time as a Democrat in substantially the same suburban district that he had represented for many years as a Republican. His reelection in that year was, therefore, a personal victory of considerable magnitude. When Robert Kennedy died, Reid made no effort to hide his hopes that Governor Rockefeller would appoint him to the Senate, but the governor chose to appoint Charles Goodell instead. Had Reid been appointed, he would very likely have won reelection to the Senate in 1970 and, in any case, he would still be a Republican today, to the benefit of the two-party system. What his future is as a Democrat, as with Lindsay, only time will tell.

For the quarter of a century from 1919 to 1943, the Democratic party held the governorship in New York State, with only one brief four-year intermission. For the next thirty-two years (counting to the end of Rockefeller's present term) the Republican party has held that office, likewise with one four-year interval. Given the historic cyclical swings of parties, the Democrats will no doubt some day regain the Executive Mansion. Whether this will be done by Lindsay or by Reid or whether it will have to await the development of new leadership and new faces are the kinds of speculations and imponderables which make politics the interesting and baffling art it is.

CHAPTER SIX

The Church

I

One afternoon during the summer after my junior year at
Princeton, I sat on the beach by the Irish Sea with my
mother's next to youngest sister. I had been bicycling in the
Tyrol with a classmate and had come over to Ireland to visit
my aunt before going home. My aunt had married an Anglo-
Irishman and she and her two small children were living
with the family while her husband was temporarily in Kenya.

I learned that afternoon that one should never say "never."
Aunt Baba was a fervent Catholic, where my mother, although deeply spiritual in her orientation, had never been
able to accept the forms and practices of the Church. Con-
sequently, neither my sister nor I had been brought up as
Catholics, and we were not practicing members of the
Church. Indeed, I had been confirmed in the Episcopal
Church while I was a student at St. Paul's School, in Concord, New Hampshire.

As Aunt Baba and I sat by the Irish Sea, I got a friendly but stern lecture about my Catholic heritage, about the teachings of the Church and about my duty with respect to both. My response was that, while I could not guess very much about my future, one thing I was sure of. That was that I would *never* become a Catholic. Five years later I was received into the Roman Catholic Church.

To be accurate, I should record that I was baptized in the Church as an infant. I can only guess that my parents must have done this to please my maternal grandmother, since, as I have said, such formal practices were not important to my mother, and my father was not a Catholic. Not only was I baptized in the Church, but I was baptized by the Right Reverend Monsignor Michael J. Lavelle, Rector of St. Patrick's Cathedral, who was a cleric to be conjured with in those days. In addition, I was baptized at home in my family's rented flat on East 56th Street, with two non-Catholic godparents. All this was very unusual in that time, but it did happen. Accordingly, after my return to the Church in later years, I could with reasonable truthfulness claim either to be a born Catholic or a convert, whichever seemed more appropriate to the occasion.

I have often been asked how it was that I became a Catholic. My answer has to be that there was no single cause or reason, but a confluence of causes and reasons, which all at once came together and formed a conviction. Catholics believe that faith is a gift, which a person can reject or neglect, but for which he cannot take credit. I believe that, and I am grateful that the Holy Spirit led me along all the many paths which brought me to the confessional and to the communion rail at the age of twenty-six.

There is no doubt that my mother, though not a practicing Catholic, had a strong influence in shaping my mind along spiritual lines. Hers was a kind of humanistic spirituality, which found its expression in good works rather than in prayer or worship. She was definitely Martha and not Mary, to cite one of Jesus's well-known parables, which was particularly appropriate since it was on the feast of that busy saint that she was born. But she believed in God, she believed in things of the spirit, and she believed that one's life was and should be affected by them.

A second influence was Dr. Samuel S. Drury, rector of St. Paul's School, which I attended between the ages of thirteen and eighteen. Dr. Drury was a rather formidable Episcopal priest who terrified most of the students at that school, but for some reason there was between him and me a warm rapport. I never found the chapel services over which he presided onerous, even though had to go every day and twice on Sundays. I believed what I heard there and I liked it. On the other hand, as was the case with almost all my fellow students, I never saw the inside of a church when I was away from school.

As I grew up I came in contact with a number of Catholics whose lives and beliefs made an impression on me. One of the things that impressed me most was that, unlike so many of my other friends, my Catholic friends took their religion seriously. They went to church on Sunday even when it was inconvenient and even when there was nobody else who would know if they did or not. They abstained from meat on Fridays, as was then required, and they lived up to dozens of other rules and regulations, some of greater significance and some of less, but most of them not easy. Obviously, their religion really mattered to them and had a controlling influence on their lives. New Year's Day is for Catholics a day on which they are obliged to go to church. I remember especially one New Year's Day when, on the way home at dawn from a convivial New Year's Eve party, the Catholics in our group stopped off to attend six o'clock mass. Very few of my non-Catholic friends would have gone to their church in similar circumstances.

People are led into the Church by a great variety of routes. For some, it is a girl or a boy with whom they fall in love. For others the road is more intellectual. Garrard Glenn, a successful New York lawyer who later taught me equity at the University of Virginia Law School, became a Catholic because of his study of history, and the example of that learned gentleman was not without its effect on me. But for me, as indicated above, it was mainly the slowly developed conviction that among Christian churches only the Catholic Church seemed to have the capacity of eliciting from its members a faithful compliance with and obedience to its teachings. I was also impressed by the diversity of those who adhered to the Church, from the most uneducated working people to some of the world's most brilliant intellects; the Church seemed to me to be Catholic with a lower case, as well as with an upper case "C."

II

Interestingly enough, my adherence to the Catholic Church, far from narrowing my theological perspective, tended to broaden it. My Catholicism caused me to reflect upon many of the accomplishments of the Protestant churches. Religion as it had been taught me at St. Paul's began to take on in retrospect values which I had not perceived while I was there. Even more importantly, I began to have an understanding of and sympathy for the Jewish religion and Jewish people that I had not previously had. The Old Testament is, of course, part of the Christian Bible, but its importance is not always made clear to Christians. It was only as I began visiting various Catholic contemplative monasteries where

176

the Psalms are said or sung in common several times a day by the monks that I began to get a real feel for the strength and beauty of the Jewish religion.

Unhappily, we live in a time when many people practice no formal religion. Since most people have deep religious instincts within them, this has led to a seeking for religion substitutes and has sometimes led to confusion between those substitutes and religion itself. The great Freud, founder of psychoanalysis, was a case in point. His contributions to the very useful science of psychiatry were of immense value, but his tendency, especially in his later years, to apply religious overtones to his scientific work was a source of confusion which has not wholly disappeared today. In this connection I had an interesting experience.

Prior to 1950 there were three separate private organizations which claimed national leadership in the field of mental health. Since manpower was limited and financial support was limited, it was deemed advisable to merge these organizations into one single group. An effort to this end was gotten underway under the leadership of Arthur H. Bunker, who had been active in the Willkie Clubs a decade earlier, and he retained me to do the necessary legal work in connection with the merger. Apparently I made a favorable impression because, when the merger had been accomplished, I was sounded out about becoming the first president of the new association. I found the prospect challenging and was prepared to accept, but then a problem developed.

The problem which developed arose out of the fact that I was a Catholic and that there were some who believed there was a fundamental conflict between the Catholic religion and psychiatry. Dr. William C. Menninger, a very great man and one of the founders of the Menninger Clinic in Topeka, Kansas, was particularly disturbed by the pros-

177

pect of having a Catholic as president of the newly merged group. His fears in this respect, as he pointed out to members of the selection committee in a series of letters, were heightened by a much publicized sermon of that time, in which a prominent Catholic priest had attacked Freudian psychoanalysis.

In the end common sense prevailed and the problem went away. I was able to persuade the selection committee that, ardent Catholic though I was, I saw no conflict between religion and psychiatry, and that I believed each should function in its own area, thereby becoming allies rather than competitors. As a consequence, I spent two exciting and productive years on leave of absence from my law firm as the first president of The National Association for Mental Health. Somewhat later, Bill Menninger invited me to join the board of the Menninger Foundation, which operated his clinic, which invitation I was honored to accept.

III

I certainly have not lived up in my conduct to the teachings of the Catholic Church. Who could? But I have believed in them and I think that I have tried to live up to them. Thus my wife and I had such children as the Lord sent us, and we did not attempt to control the number by artificial means. Although we lived in a community where most of our friends sent their children to non-sectarian schools, our children went to the local Catholic parochial school. Maybe the nuns who taught them did not have M.A.'s from Harvard and maybe the economics of the parish required that there be fifty pupils in each classroom, but what did that matter compared with exposure to the teachings of the Church? I used to tell my children that I considered it more important that they get into heaven than that they get into an Ivy League college. I have no regrets about those decisions.

The Church today is, if course, going through a period of great change and uncertainty. The kind of obedience and compliance with its teachings which first attracted me to it are not as widespread as they were when I came in. Not only are the ties of obedience weakening among the membership, but they are weakening even among the clergy and, in some cases, among the bishops themselves. All this is very troublesome to many, and especially to people who came to the Church by choice rather than by birth. For such people, the Catholic Church is now the victim of the very looseness and lack of discipline which caused them to leave their own church in the first place. For some of these people, there is real disillusion.

Happily that has not been the case with me. Many of the changes which have taken place since the Second Vatican Council I welcome. The pendulum had swung much too far toward centralized, hierarchical authority and toward a substitution of religiosity, almost even of superstition in extreme circumstances, for the kind of faith in which the intellect and the will play a reasonable role. Thus the developments of Vatican II, in my view, were clearly needed and healthy.

The awe in which the hierarchy of the pre-conciliar Church was held in some quarters is exemplified by a story concerning Charles Hanson Towne, who was a well-known New York journalist and man-about-town in the early part of the century. The story was told to me by my mother, who was a friend of Towne's and who got it from him.

Finding himself in Rome, Charlie Towne decided he would like to have an audience with the pope, who was then Pius XI. Although not a Catholic, as a journalist he was

179

interested in the pope as a figure of importance and influence. The United States ambassador in Rome, who was his friend, agreed to obtain a ticket for him.

As it turned out, Towne received not one ticket but two for an audience the following day. Accordingly, he invited an American friend who was in Rome to come with him. The friend, who was also a non-Catholic, was reluctant to go. He indicated that his objection arose out of the fact that one ordinarily genuflects to the pope and that he regarded such obiesance as somehow un-American. Towne, who wanted his friend's company, finally persuaded him that there was no requirement that he genuflect and that the pope would no doubt be satisfied with a good American handshake or a simple bow. The friend finally agreed to go, but only on the understanding that he would not "bend the knee to any foreign potentate." Towne said that he fully understood, that he would not be embarrassed by whatever greeting his friend chose to give, and the following morning they went together to the Vatican. Little did he know what was in store.

They were part of what is known as a "special audience." There are general audiences, in which the pope appears and speaks before a large group but does not talk individually with any of those present. At the other extreme is the private audience in the pope's study. This is generally reserved for very high ranking government or ecclesiastical personages. In between is the special audience. In the special audience people gather in small groups in a large room, the groups ordinarily being made up of persons who arrived together, such as members of a single family. The pope then moves from group to group, talking privately with each group for whatever time seems appropriate. My wife and I had such an audience with Pius XII, and my two oldest sons and I had such an audience with John XXIII.

On the morning in question, Towne and his friend constituted one group, and were placed near the portal through which the pope would enter. Other groups were scattered about the room. Suddenly the door opened and the pope came in, clad in solid white except for his scarlet shoes, with a simple gold cross pending on his chest. Before Towne knew what was happening, his friend rushed forward toward the approaching pontiff, cast himself prostrate on the floor and attempted to kiss the pope's toe. So astonished was the pope that he withdrew his foot, with the consequence that the friend kissed the floor.

In due course, everybody regained his outward composure, but the incident was not one to be forgotten by any person present. There is, of course, an ancient tradition, long ago abandoned, of kissing the pope's toe. The faithful also sometimes kiss the toe of a marble statue of St. Peter located in St. Peter's Basilica next door to the Vatican Palace. In his anxiety not to humble himself unduly, Charlie Towne's friend simply got confused.

IV

Perhaps my capacity to "roll with the punches" of the modern Church is due, in part at least, to the influence on my life of two very great priests. I have known many very great priests, and each of them has helped me at one time or another in my spiritual and temporal struggles, but of them all there were two who had the greatest influence at critical moments of my life. One was Father Leonard Feeney, the other Father James Keller.

Father Feeney is a member of the Society of Jesus, commonly known as Jesuits. Subsequent to my acquaintance with him, he pursued a course which resulted in his formal

181

censure by his superiors. In my relationship with him, however, there was no indication of the troubles which lay ahead. It was to him that I went for instruction when I decided that I wanted to become a Catholic.

I had been introduced to Father Feeney by a very attractive girl whom he had previously instructed. She was engaged to marry my cousin who was a Catholic and, although it was not by any means necessary for her to enter the Church in order to be married, she had concluded that she wished to do so. As the time for her marriage came closer, she became increasingly impatient to become a Catholic because she wanted to be married at a nuptial mass in church. In those days the rules of the Church, while fully permitting marriages between Catholics and non-Catholics, reserved the nuptial mass to those situations where both parties were Catholic.

The young lady pressed the matter of timing so strongly that Father Feeney had to address himself to it. Obviously, he was pleased by her wish to accelerate her entrance into the Church. On the other hand, he was concerned that her decision was perhaps too much affected by her emotions and by her wish for the color and the ceremony of the mass. Accordingly, his response to her pressure was to advise her to wait, to wait not for the marriage but for the conversion. He said that he would be happy to marry her on schedule, but not in church and not at a mass. Then, after she had come back from the wedding trip, if she still wanted to become a Catholic, he would receive her into the Church and then there could be the nuptial mass which she so ardently desired. The alternative, he said, and the only one, was to postpone the wedding.

The response from the young lady was that so firmly did she wish to be married at a nuptial mass, that if the wedding had to be postponed she would postpone it. That was enough for Father Feeney. Hearing that, he replied that he would baptize her the next day. She had her nuptial mass and to this day she is a faithful and indeed an apostolic Catholic.

As is clear from the foregoing story, one of Father Feeney's great attributes was his wisdom. His greatest attribute, however, and the one which so greatly influenced me, was his charity. In the way in which Catholics use the word, charity does not have anything to do with charity balls or charity drives as they appear on the society pages of the newspapers; charity in the Catholic lexicon means love.

The proof of Father Feeney's charity, so far as I was concerned, was his treatment of the subject of mortal sin. According to Catholic doctrine, to be mortal (that is, to seriously separate a person from God) a sin must comprise three elements: it must be an important matter; the sinner must know that it is an important matter; and it must be done with the full consent of the will. In Father Feeney's view, the accumulation of all three of these factors would be a virtual impossibility, at least for a person of good intentions. Indeed, he used to say, how could anybody of good intentions give full consent to any act which he knew was both important and wrong? There will be those who disagree with what he said, but there can be few who fail to recognize the charity implicit in what he said. What he said is something I deeply believe, which is that sins of the flesh, sins of passion, sins of weakness, are rarely mortal. If there is a mortal sin, it is a sin of the intellect and of the will.

Father James Keller is very different from Father Feeney. Father Keller is a member of Maryknoll, a society of missionary priests. As the founder of The Christophers, he was an ecumenist before his time. His television shows, his books, and his newsletter "Christopher Notes" have brought him significant recognition in non-Catholic as well as in Catholic circles. The motto of The Christophers is "It is better to light one candle than to curse the darkness." Father Keller believes that small personal acts, by their cumulative effect, can change the world. He believes that if each person, regardless of race, creed or color, would "light a candle" for good and for the Lord, the world would be a better place to live in.

I met Father Keller shortly after I became a Catholic and I played a small role in helping design the original shape of The Christophers' effort. However, the role he played in my life was more important than that, and it tied in with Father Feeney. In the winter of 1946, I visited Father Feeney at St. Benedict's Center, which was a private Catholic student center near Harvard College in Cambridge. While I was there, Father Feeney took me out to Roxbury to visit Sister Mary of the Blessed Sacrament, who was a nun in a Carmelite Monastery in that Boston suburb. The Carmelites are a religious order of great strictness. Today there has been some relaxation, but in those days the nuns of that order not only never left the monastery for any reason but could talk with visitors only heavily veiled and only from behind a grille; their life was (and to a very large degree still is) one of prayer and penance for the sins and sufferings of the world. It is told that when John Carroll of Maryland was named the first native bishop in the United States, he asked first for a community of Carmelites. First the prayers, he said, then after that let there come the teaching nuns and the nursing nuns and the others of more "practical" vocations.

Sister Mary of the Blessed Sacrament had been a Jew and, as I was told, a very beautiful and highly educated woman. Finding no satisfaction in the pleasures of secular life, however, and not finding the answers she needed in her own faith, she had been led to Father Feeney, who helped her

184

become a Catholic. After that she joined the Carmelites and went to Roxbury.

We had a nice talk that afternoon although, as a first-time visitor to a Carmelite house, I was a little nervous. As we rose to leave, Father Feeney asked Sister Mary to pray for me and to pray especially that I would be the first Catholic president of the United States. It was a silly request and I should perhaps have ignored it, but I did not.

I was then nearly thirty-five years old and unmarried. I had had many women friends but, partly perhaps because of the war and my five years with the Navy, I had never gotten married. So I responded to Father Feeney's request by asking Sister to pray not for what Father Feeney had asked but to pray instead that I would meet the girl that I should marry and that she would be Catholic. In view of how much the Catholic faith meant to me and of the importance that I attached to marriage, I was asking for help in having these two important factors coincide. As it turned out, her prayers were more effective than I could have dared to hope.

It was a few weeks later that I received a telephone call from Father Keller asking me if I would join him at a public dinner on a Sunday night to celebrate the hundred and twenty-fifth anniversary of the independence of Greece. My response was that much as I liked Father Keller and much as I would enjoy seeing him, a public dinner on a Sunday night was just too much. But he did not give in easily. This was to be a very special occasion, he said, and, besides, we would be sitting at the table of Spyros Skouras, a very great man. I did not know Mr. Skouras, but I had heard of him as a stimulating and interesting person, so I accepted. As it turned out Mr. Skouras was on the dais, so I never did meet him, at least not that night. But I did meet his oldest daughter who was at our table. Shortly thereafter we became engaged and a few months after that we were married at a nuptial mass at which Father Leonard Feeney was the celebrant. Father Keller, of course, was in the sanctuary.

Last year I had lunch with Father Keller. He is old now and not too well. He asked me what I thought of the world situation. I gave him a reply which was somewhat pessimistic—what other view can an ordinary person have in this troubled world? He paused a moment and then said, "What a wonderful circumstance for the Lord to function in." That may sound Pollyanna-ish to some, but from Father Keller's viewpoint it is not. That is the kind of thinking which has motivated him for all his more than seventy years and has made him such a force for good.

V

When I say that I accept the changes which have taken place in the Catholic Church since Vatican II, and, indeed, that I welcome many of those changes as long overdue, that is not to say that I welcome everything that has happened in the Church in recent years. I welcome the increasing engagement of the intellect in the affairs of the Church, but not the lessening of discipline. I welcome the enlarged emphasis on love for one's fellow man, but not the forgetting that the reason for loving one's fellow man is that he is created in the image and likeness of God. I welcome the developing acceptance by the clergy, including the ordered clergy, that spiritual salvation cannot be isolated from considerations of poverty and prejudice and war, but I regret the tendency in some quarters to forget the importance of prayer and penance and sacrifice.

The simple fact is that Jesus Christ gave mankind the

answer to all its problems, if only his rules would be followed. It was Chesterton who said that the trouble with Christianity is not that it has been tried and found wanting but that it has been found hard and never tried. This is not to say that Christianity is the only religion by which God has manifested himself to the world. At least in my view, that is not necessarily so. It seems to me that the fact of Christianity's being true for part of the world's people is not necessarily inconsistent with God's having manifested himself by other means and through other philosophies to other parts of the world's people. However, the point is that for those hundreds of millions of us who have been exposed to Christ's teachings during the last two thousand years, that is God's way of communicating with us. And the rules which Christ gave us would in fact bring us happiness and peace and salvation if only we had enough sense to follow them. The Sermon on the Mount and many numbers of parables point the way, to say nothing of dozens of explicit directives and utterances. What could be more explicit, for example, than "Whosoever shall save his life shall lose it, and whosoever shall lose his life for my sake shall find it"? Or St. Peter's ringing response when Jesus asked his apostles whom they believed him to be: "Thou art Christ, the son of the living God." Not a good man, not a social leader, not a prophet, but Christ, the son of God. We read, we hear, but we do not take heed.

Twenty years ago, long before the current turbulence in the Church, I stated that there were three people in the world I would like to meet. As it happened, they were all women: Barbara Ward, Maria von Trapp, and Dorothy Day. Since then, I have met Barbara Ward and have had the opportunity of knowing Maria von Trapp moderately well. Although Dorothy Day, alas, remains for me a personality of the printed page, she has nevertheless had almost as great an effect on me as if I had met her. Today, twenty years later, these three women still represent for me much of what is great in the world and in the Church. Although each of them is a forceful and fiercely independent individual, and although each of them has been deeply aware of the Church's limitations in dealing with some of the material problems of our material world, nevertheless all three have remained faithful members of the institutional Church.

Barbara Ward's intellect is probably the equal of any other living person's. An economist of great distinction, she has made a specialty of exposing in ringing prose the plight of the third world and the imbalance between those who possess the goods of this planet and those who do not. Nineteen years after its first publication, her *Faith and Freedom* is still one of the great historical expositions of our Christian European civilization. She is a world citizen of the first rank and a Catholic who sets an example to be followed.

Maria von Trapp is very different. She was a young nun in Austria when she was called from the convent to take care of a family of children whose mother had died. As the central figure in the Broadway play and the motion picture *The Sound of Music,* her story is too well known to be repeated here in detail. She and her husband and their children fled the Nazi tyranny and came to the United States. A family singing group which they had originally formed in Europe continued on a larger scale here and soon became world famous under the name The Trapp Family Singers.

What is not so well known about the Baroness von Trapp, however, are the trials and tribulations of her life in later years. Plagued by accidents and illness herself, there have also been deaths and other sadnesses among her children. Although her autobiography became one of the most successful Broadway plays and motion pictures in theatrical history, her ignorance of the legal niceties resulted in her getting a much smaller monetary return from those triumphs than a shrewder person might have received. Yet through all those vicissitudes, she has never lost her Catholic faith, her zest for life, or her desire to be of service to others. Moreover, the winds which have blown through the window which Pope John XXIII opened when he summoned the Second Vatican Council to Rome may have ruffled her Austrian dirndl, but they never ruffled her calm acceptance of the fact that the Church and the world, in the last analysis, are guided not by man but by the Holy Spirit. To spend an evening with Maria von Trapp, as my wife and I do from time to time, is to be lifted up and to be made aware of how minor are the connections between material well-being and true happiness.

Undoubtedly there are many saints in the world today. Almost certainly Dorothy Day, seventy-six years old, is one of them. She began life as a Marxist, living and working among the poor. Then one day, in a west side bar in New York, she heard Eugene O'Neill recite Francis Thompson's great ode, "The Hound of Heaven." Francis Thompson was a destitute narcotics addict who lived in penury in the slums of Victorian London, and that work sings as only divine inspiration could make it sing.

It would be foolish to suggest that the hearing of a poem, however great, could by itself change a person's life, and her writings make it clear that Dorothy Day was moved by more than that. But it is recorded that that recital did play a part in what followed, and a west side bar was just the right place for her to hear it. In any event, it was shortly thereafter that she became a Catholic. The full story of her conversion is written in two of her books, *From Union Square to Rome* and *The Long Loneliness,* and her philosophy is propounded in other books and in the *Catholic Worker,* of which she was the founder. Poor by choice, a convicted criminal for causes in which she volunteered because she believed them to be above the law, she has always accepted the legal consequences and penalites of her illegal acts. Even more importantly, she has remained a staunch and loyal member of the established Church. As John Cogley wrote in *The New York Times* on the occasion of her seventy-fifth birthday, "Dorothy Day not only changed her friends and admirers, she changed American Catholicism itself. And she did it by 'working within the system.' Don't look for her in the Underground Church. You are more likely to find her kneeling in the shadows at one of those friendly little churches on the Lower East Side."

There are some who believe the Church will not survive, that its present turbulence signals its dissolution and that it is on the way out. I am confident that is not the case. Christ told us that his Church would survive for all time, and I believe it will. Just as the pendulum swung too far in one direction before Vatican II, maybe it is now swinging too far in the other direction. If so, it will come back.

The crisis is not primarily a crisis in the Church in any case. The lack of discipline in modern society, the absence of a sense of direction, the undue emphasis on material values, the selfishness—these are not crises of the Church as such, but of the Atlantic world. Probably our Atlantic civilization will someday perish, as all civilizations in the past have eventually perished. If and when that happens, the Church as a part of that civilization must of course be affected. But the whole world will not be destroyed and the Church is everywhere in the world. Just as some new civilization will in due course rise again from some other part of the world—maybe from Africa, where the radioactive winds resulting from a nuclear holocaust in the northern hemishere would be less destructive—so the Church will rise again. Indeed, the fact that the Church today is showing some of its greatest vitality in the area of the African subcontinent may be more than a coincidence.

CHAPTER SEVEN

Three Famous Airmen

I

In the course of this book I have alluded from time to time to my mother. Partly this is because my mother and father were divorced when I was ten years old and it was with my mother that I lived until I was married. But it is also because my mother was a very unusual woman. Among her accomplishments there was one of special interest: by piloting Santos Dumont's airship Number Nine across the Bois de Boulogne in 1903, she became the first woman in the world to solo a powered aircraft. It was indirectly through my mother that I met and became good friends with Charles A. Lindbergh, who in 1927 was the first person to fly solo across the Atlantic Ocean. Spyros Skouras, my wife's dynamic and extraordinary father, was the source of my encounter with Howard Hughes, the third famous airman discussed in this chapter.

191

My father's father and grandfather, both having the name Oren, as did my father himself, were professors of mathematics at Hamilton College in Clinton, New York, a small village near the city of Utica in the beautiful valley of the Mohawk River. The first Oren was known to his students as Cube Root and the second as Square Root. My father was born in Columbia, Missouri, where his father was teaching for the summer, but he was brought up in Clinton, where he lived until he graduated from Hamilton College.

Upon graduating, my father came to New York City to make his living, since there were few opportunities in Clinton and further financial help from his family was out of the question. My father was one of five children and raising them had strained his professor father's small earnings to the limit. Through his uncle, Elihu Root, who was already making a name at the New York Bar, my father got a job with the Metropolitan Street Railroad Company, starting as a conductor. A few years later, when he was still only twenty-eight years old, he had risen to the position of general manager of that company, which, at that time, was the largest public utility in the world.

For reasons having nothing to do with its operations, which was where my father's responsibilities lay, the company later went into receivership. For a time my father continued to manage it for the receivers, but ultimately that came to an end and there was a period during which he was unemployed. Both because of his nature and because neither he nor my mother had any financial resources, this was a very difficult period in his life. Indeed, although I was too young to have much memory of the happenings of those days, I have always believed that the strains put upon the marriage by that episode of unemployment were part of the cause of its failure.

Ultimately my father was elected president of the Hudson

and Manhattan Railroad Company, which operated the trains which ran under the Hudson River between Manhattan and New Jersey. He retired from that post in 1930 and lived quietly in retirement until his death eighteen years later. After our parents' divorce, my sister and I lived mainly with my mother, but we saw my father regularly. He was a shy man and in his later years was not well, so that there were limits to what he and his children could do together. I have always been grateful, however, that he lived long enough to know my wife and to see our first son, who carries his name.

My mother was a very different kind of person. Her father and mother, both of full Spanish blood, came to New York from Cuba and were married in 1870. My mother was the fourth of eight children of that marriage, whose names were Joachim, Rita, Ricardo, Aida, Maria, Enrique, Angelica (nicknamed Baba), and Mercedes. All brilliant, all handsome or beautiful, my mother and her sisters and brothers cut a swathe which was in striking contrast to the simple teachers, lawyers, and small entrepreneurs from whom my father was descended. Drawn by Helleu, painted by Sargent, Zuloaga, and Boldini, sculpted by Malvina Hoffman, the deAcosta women were among the most celebrated personages of the relatively limited "society" of the late nineteenth and early twentieth centuries.

Yet the life which my mother ultimately chose to lead was conservative in style and largely devoted to the service of others. Because of her beauty and her intelligence, she could easily have married into wealth and high social position. Indeed, at various times her hand was sought by men in those categories. But my mother chose instead to accept the proposal of my father, who was handsome and intelligent, but certainly neither rich nor highly placed, at least by the standards of "society."

One of the extraordinary facts about my mother is that she earned her own living until she was seventy-five years old. After her divorce from my father she got a paid job doing public relations work for the American Child Health Association, of which Herbert Hoover was chairman. In a later period she became the chairman of the Municipal Art Committee, in which position she helped Mayor LaGuardia channel some of the money which was being spent for relief during the Great Depression into constructive projects. Her last job was executive director of the Eye Bank for Sight Restoration, which she helped found. The principal mission of that group was to facilitate the donations of corneas from the eyes of the dead for transplant into the eyes of the living.

My mother's final job was especially appropriate because for the last forty years of her life she was almost totally blind. As a result of the emotional strain resulting from her divorce from my father, she became a victim of glaucoma at a time when very little was known about that disease. She underwent a series of operations performed by Dr. William Holland Wilmer, who at the time was practicing ophthalmology in Washington, D.C. Those operations resulted in the saving of a small fraction of the vision of one eye. Subsequently, she led a campaign which raised several million dollars to establish the William Holland Wilmer Institute at Johns Hopkins University, which, at the time, was the only institution of its kind in the United States.

The fact that my mother earned her living until the age of seventy-five gave rise to an amusing incident related to her claim for social security. Under what has always seemed to me a very unwise law, a person cannot draw social security benefits if that person earns more than a certain annual income. But upon reaching the age of seventy-two this limitation is no longer operative. Some time after my mother

194

reached that age, I drew this fact to her attention and advised her that, even though she was still working, she was entitled to social security benefits retroactive to the age of seventy-two. There was a problem, however, which had to be overcome. The problem was that we had to prove my mother's age and, since all her life until she was past seventy she had lied about it, this was no easy task. The obvious first attempt was to find a birth certificate. I wrote to the state of New Jersey, where she was born, and received a certificate in reply. But, alas, the certificate was made out simply for "Acosta-female" without any further identification. Since there were five female Acostas of various ages in my mother's family, this was not proof enough to meet the requirements of governmental red tape.

Next I tried St. Patrick's Cathedral for a baptismal certificate, but with no success. I then decided to get her marriage certificate for her marriage to my father, confident that she must have told the truth about her age at that early stage. I found the certificate, but even then the statement as to age was false by three critical years. Frustrated beyond words, I confronted my mother. "Mother," I said, "your lifetime of prevarication is now costing you two thousand dollars tax free." Her reply at the age of seventy-four, which I shall never forget, was "It was worth it."

The spirit which made that reply possible at the age of seventy-four was the same spirit which caused her at the age of twenty-two to be the first woman in the world ever to fly a powered aircraft solo. Her opportunity to do so arose out of her acquaintance with Alberto Santos Dumont. Santos Dumont was a Brazilian of independent means who lived in Paris at the turn of the century. His primary interest in life lay in building powered airships. Free-floating balloons had been experimented with since the Mongolphier brothers had ascended in a hot air balloon at Versailles in the presence of

Louis XIV, but until Santos Dumont nobody had ever been successful in directing them effectively. Starting in the year 1898, Santos Dumont built a series of powered balloons which he was able to direct at speeds up to fifteen miles an hour. In 1903 he produced his Number Nine, otherwise known as his Runabout. In a way it was the precursor of the helicopter, because it was small and highly maneuverable. It had room for only one person, Santos Dumont himself, and the basket in which he was conveyed was constructed to contain his five foot five inch body and no more.

How my mother met Santos Dumont I do not know, but her family normally spent their summers in France and, knowing my mother's spirit, it was not surprising that she was among those who used to gather at the airfield in Neuilly, on the outskirts of Paris, which was Santos Dumont's base. As she got to know him she one day expressed a desire to take Number Nine aloft herself. "But mademoiselle," he replied, "we would have to await a day when the flag at the summit of the Eiffel Tower is lying limp." As it turned out there came such a day, and on that day my mother appeared at Neuilly. Santos Dumont was as good as his word and he allowed her to take the ship up. There was a problem in fitting her clothes-padded turn of the century hips into the small basket, but somehow she squeezed them in.

It happened that on that day there was an international polo game in progress at Bagatelle on the other side of the Bois de Boulogne. My mother piloted the airship to the polo field and descended. The crowd believed it to be Santos Dumont, which was exciting enough. Finally, perceiving that it was a woman, they broke into cheers. In due course Santos Dumont himself arrived, having pedaled there on his bicycle. As he approached my mother he cried, "Mademoiselle, you are the first woman aviator in the world." All this was four months before the Wright brothers flew at Kitty Hawk.

Incidentally, my mother finally did get her social security payments. Through the help of a young lawyer in my office, we located a baptismal certificate in a small church on the Jersey shore, which carried her correct name and date of birth. So in the end she had her cake and ate it too.

II

No event in modern times has caught the imagination of the country to the extent that Charles A. Lindbergh's solo flight to Paris did in 1927. Aviation by that time had developed to a point where such a flight was technically possible, and there were a number of individuals and groups contemplating trying it. Raymond Orteig of New York City had offered a $25,000 prize for the first person to accomplish that objective, subject to certain rules and conditions.

Among those hoping to win the prize was Lindbergh, then only twenty-five years old. He was successful in getting a group of businessmen in St. Louis to back him financially, and he had ordered a small monoplane powered by a single 220 horsepower engine. But in addition to his financial and technical problems he was faced with serious competition from others. There were half a dozen groups organizing for the same objective, including one headed by Lieutenant Commander Richard E. Byrd, who earlier had commanded the first successful expedition to fly to the North Pole.

Then suddenly on May 20 Lindbergh took off from Roosevelt Field on Long Island in his small plane, the *Spirit of St. Louis,* headed for Paris. What set the imagination of the country and of the world on fire is hard to say. In part it was no doubt the drama of the race, with most of Lindbergh's competitors being better known and better financed, so that he represented a kind of underdog quality which has always appealed to the American public. There was also his youth and his extraordinary good looks. Most important of all, perhaps, was the fact that he was flying alone in a tiny plane with only one engine. The risks were enormous and, as the hours passed following his takeoff, hundreds of millions prayed for his success.

By the time he landed in Paris thirty-three and a half hours later, he was a hero of the first magnitude. Vast crowds met him at the airport and later at the airports in Brussels and London, where he flew for short visits and resplendent receptions. President Coolidge sent a cruiser, the USS *Memphis,* to bring him and the plane back to the United States and he later received the Congressional Medal of Honor. Upon returning to the United States, Lindbergh undertook a series of good-will flights to seventy-five cities around the country and to Latin America for the purpose of promoting understanding of and enthusiasm for aviation. The *Spirit of St. Louis* ended up in the Smithsonian Institution in Washington, D.C., where, interestingly enough, another of the aeronautical exhibits is the engine of Santos Dumont's Number Nine, together with photographs of my mother's flight.

Great and explosive as was the initial reaction to the Paris flight it was heightened further by Lindbergh's conduct and bearing. Besieged by offers and contracts for motion pictures and for sponsorships of one kind or another, he turned them all down. His simple dignity in the presence of the leaders of governments and others by whom he was received was captivating beyond words. There was also about him something of that magic combination of avoiding publicity and at the same time conducting himself in such a manner as subtly to attract it which, especially when it is uncontrived, is one of the most powerful of public relations forces. Others who have demonstrated comparable magic in other periods and in different circumstances have been Greta Garbo, the actress, Jacqueline Kennedy Onassis, and Howard Hughes.

My family did not know Lindbergh at the time of his flight, but they met him very shortly thereafter. My mother was a long-time friend of Mrs. Harry F. Guggenheim, whose husband was active in the field of aviation and in contact with Lindbergh. Realizing that Lindbergh needed legal advice and help, Guggenheim recommended Henry Breckinridge, a brilliant and attractive New York attorney whom my mother married that year. Through that association my family came to know Lindbergh well, and for more than a year between early 1928 and his marriage to Anne Morrow in the spring of 1929, my family's apartment was his New York City base. Not only did he and I share a bedroom during the times that we were both at home, but on several occasions when I needed them he loaned me the beautiful evening clothes Ambassador Herrick had had made for him in Paris. Since he and I were of similar builds, I fitted easily into them. Needless to say, the fact of my wearing them added greatly to my popularity on the party circuit that year.

I first met Lindbergh when I came home from boarding school for spring vacation in March 1928. By that time he had acquired a slightly larger plane built by the same company that had built the *Spirit of St. Louis*. He was planning a trip to Washington, and I was told that I could go along. I had never flown, and my excitement at the age of seventeen at the prospect of making my first flight with the World's greatest hero can hardly be overstated.

We took off from Curtiss Field on Long Island early in the morning of March 20. The plane had room for a pilot and four passengers. The passengers, in addition to myself, were Major Thomas G. Lanphier, commander of the First Pursuit Group at Selfridge Field in Michigan, who was a close friend of Lindbergh's and whose son later had an outstanding record in the Air Force during World War II; Rear Admiral Emory Land, a cousin of Lindbergh's on his mother's side; and Henry Breckinridge, my stepfather. The plane was built to cruise at about one hundred miles an hour, which should have gotten us to Washington in two hours. There were strong head winds, however, with the consequence that we moved across the ground at a slower speed. A more serious consequence, so far as I was concerned, was that the head winds created a certain amount of air turbulence, and the light plane was bouncing around rather roughly. Partly because of that and partly, no doubt, because of the excitement of my first flight, I suddenly realized that I was going to be sick. There was no means of opening the window and I was at a loss as to what to do, until my stepfather suggested my hat. It was an expensive receptacle, but I had no choice except to use it and then to dispose of it. Strange as it may seem in this day of high speed, pressurized aircraft, the means by which I disposed of it was simply to open the door of the plane beside me and drop it out. It is not pleasant to remember even at this late date, but it must be recorded that before we arrived in Washington three hours after takeoff I had similarly used the hat of every person in the plane, including the hat of its distinguished pilot. In Washington there was a large luncheon scheduled in Lindbergh's honor by the commander of Bolling Field, through which I sat with some difficulty.

The purpose of Lindbergh's trip to Washington was to offer short flights over that city to members of the Congress. Aviation was still very young at the time and many persons were afraid of flying. Few could resist an invitation to fly with Lindbergh, however, and he deemed it his duty to give the members of Congress this educational opportunity. He used two planes for the purpose, a Fokker and a Ford, both tri-motored planes, and the flights continued for a number of days. As he was taking a group up over Washington in one of the planes, the other plane was loaded with new passengers, so as to be ready for a quick takeoff as soon as the first plane came down and the pilot switched over. The passengers were clothed in air suits and provided with parachutes. I do not know whether the latter were required by regulation or whether they were simply a means of adding to the drama of the occasion.

Where I got to know Lindbergh really well, however, was in Princeton. He and his charming and talented wife first rented a house in the outskirts of Princeton itself. Later, they bought a large tract of land and built a new house near Hopewell, about fifteen miles southwest of Princeton. While I was a student at Princeton, the Lindberghs generously invited me out for many weekends, first at the house in Princeton and later at the house in Hopewell.

I greatly enjoyed those weekends. Both Charles and Anne Lindbergh were stimulating, and I gained a great deal from their company. Although Lindbergh had made a good deal of money from his writing and from his consulting work, and although Anne Lindbergh was a member of the wealthy Morrow family, they lived simply. They did this because they liked it that way and also because they thought it was right. They did have a couple taking care of them, but Lindbergh was careful to justify this luxury on the ground that it freed him and his wife to do creative things which they could not have done if they were tied down to housekeeping. The implication was that if they could not have philosophically justified having the couple they would not have had them.

There were a number of amusing episodes during my weekend visits. One which I remember proves that even a person with Lindbergh's strong technical background is not technically infallible. A central humidifying system had been installed in the Hopewell house at a time when that kind of device was relatively new and untried. Lindbergh was very proud of it and went out of his way to explain to me how much healthier it was to live during the winter in a properly humidified house. It so happened that I was there the first time that the system was tried. When we woke up the next morning, the walls and all the furniture were soaking wet. Lindbergh had lowered the furnace thermostat for the night, forgetting that this would raise the relative humidity and cause the moisture in the air to precipitate.

It was from the house in Hopewell that the Lindberghs' first child, then only eighteen months old, was kidnapped on the night of Tuesday, March 1, 1932. On that evening I had been attending a late class on the Princeton campus. On my way back to my room I stopped to have a visit with Fife Symington, one of my classmates, who later in life was appointed by President Nixon as his ambassador to Trinidad and Tobago. As I entered Fife Symington's room, he told me that he had just heard on the radio that the Lindbergh baby had been kidnapped from the house in Hopewell. In those days there were many false stories and rumors about the Lindberghs, and I was confident that this was one of them. I had spent the previous weekend in Hopewell and when I left on Sunday night I knew that the family was planning to return early the next morning to the Morrow house in Englewood, where they generally spent the middle part of the week. Clearly, therefore, the story about the baby's having been kidnapped from Hopewell was untrue. I went back to my room and went to sleep without concern.

At two o'clock the next morning there was a violent

knocking on my door. I rose to find Henry Breckinridge, my stepfather, who had driven down from New York and who stopped at my room to ask me to direct him to the Lindbergh house. The reason, of course, was that the Lindbergh baby had in fact been kidnapped and he, as Lindbergh's lawyer, was needed. What had happened was that the baby woke up on Monday morning with a cold, thereby causing the family to change its plans and stay an extra two days in Hopewell. There are many mysteries about the tragic event which are still unsolved. One of them is how the kidnapper could have known of that last-minute change of plans.

Except to suffer for my famous friends who were undergoing such trials and tribulations, I had very little contact with the search for the kidnapped child and with the subsequent search for his kidnapper. There is one episode, however, which I do remember. In the course of the search for the child, a number of individuals prominent in the organized underworld offered their services to Lindbergh, and persons in Lindbergh's entourage came to know some of those underworld figures reasonably well. As a consequence, I was taken one night to dine with one of the leading underworld figures of the day in his penthouse on the west side of Manhattan. Our host of the evening filled my young ears with fantastic tales about the organization of that segment of society. According to him, there existed in the underworld a veritable governmental structure, with representatives of various underworld geographical or industry interests meeting together, very much as national leaders meet today in the United Nations. Through those meetings, most of the jurisdictional disputes between various underworld chieftains were settled by negotiation, and it was only when negotiation failed that the kind of open warfare broke out which made the newspaper headlines. It was because that underworld organization wanted to make plain that it had had no part in the kidnapping that some of its members made their services available in the search for the child. As we sat and talked in the penthouse that evening, we could look across the street and see a brewery belonging to our host operating at full blast and in full public view, although this was still more than a year before the repeal of the Eighteenth Amendment.

In the course of my many conversations with Lindbergh, I became convinced that he would some day take a major public position on some major issue. He was aware of his enormous influence in the country and in the world, and he was carefully harboring it, so it seemed to me, for some occasion worthy of its expenditure. As it turned out, that occasion was his effort in the year 1941 to keep the United States out of the war in Europe. Lindbergh's father, who had emigrated from Sweden to the United States at an early age, later became a lawyer and a member of Congress from Minnesota. When World War I was officially declared in 1917, Congressman Lindbergh cast his vote in the negative. To what extent that act by the father had an effect upon the son, once can only surmise. Beyond that, Lindbergh's technical knowledge of aviation made it natural that he should have been impressed by the power and efficiency of Hitler's *Luftwaffe*, which he had visited and seen at first hand. In any case, he came to the conclusion that the interests of the United States would not be advanced by challenging the German aggression in Europe and, operating in part through an organization known as America First, he devoted all his very great talents and prestige to keeping the country out of the war.

Those were difficult days in the United States and they were particularly difficult for the Lindbergh family. Anne Lindbergh's father had been a partner in J. P. Morgan & Co., the great international banking house, as well as ambassador to Mexico. The views of the Morrow family and of those with whom members of that family generally associated were in substantial conflict with the position taken by Lindbergh. Somehow, Lindbergh and his wife worked this difficulty out, however, and certainly so far as the public was aware, there was never any division between them.

It was in this general connection that I had my last long talk with Lindbergh. In early 1941, he had not yet totally committed himself to his antiwar crusade, but it was clear from public reports that he was tending in that direction. As a disciple of Wendell Willkie, I felt very much the other way. Accordingly, I invited myself to spend an evening with him in the house in which he and his family were then living in Cold Spring Harbor on Long Island.

Lindbergh met me at the train. Since it was pouring rain when we arrived at his house, he let me out at the front door, saying that he would put the car in the garage and meet me inside. I ran up the front steps, burst open the door, and slammed it behind me. What I then saw made my blood run cold. After the kidnapping, the Lindberghs had acquired a police dog named Thor, for the god of thunder, which was trained to protect the household. As the front door slammed behind me, I saw the dog, large and terrifying, standing between me and the staircase leading to the second floor. There was nobody else in the hall. I was afraid to call out, I was certainly afraid to move, and with the closed door behind me there was no retreat. I simply stood there for what seemed an eternity, with the dog standing tense and immobile a few feet away, until Lindbergh came in from the garage. He laughed as though the whole thing was a big joke, and assured me that I had been in no danger so long as I had not tried to go upstairs.

We had a stimulating and interesting conversation that

evening, during which I advanced such arguments as I could in favor of giving military aid to England, which was then fighting alone. Lindbergh's mind was clearly made up the other way, however, and I got nowhere. He was convinced that England, like France, which had already fallen, was weak and decadent. He was also of the belief that there would be other enemies in later periods of history who would be a much greater threat to the United States than Germany and that we should husband our resources for that later struggle. Soon thereafter, he made his position public and waged a strenuous campaign in support of it right up to the Japanese attack at Pearl Harbor. After that attack and during the war, he served his country loyally and effectively, both at home and in various theaters of combat.

There are very few people who could have been subjected to the adulation to which Lindbergh was subjected following his Paris flight and have survived. The kinds of temptations, material and spiritual, which accompanied that adulation would have destroyed any young man of twenty-five years who did not have unusual stability and strength of character. Lindbergh had both in large measure. Not only did he survive that adulation, but he survived the tragedy of the kidnapping and the later bitterness surrounding his campaign to keep the United States out of war. After the death of his first son, he and his wife raised five more children and he devoted his very great talents and energy to writing, to conservation and, of course, to the continued development of aviation. His wife, for her part, in addition to being wife and mother, became one of the most noted nonfiction authors of her day. Charles and Anne Lindbergh have been major forces for good in the difficult world in which they have lived, and I will always be grateful for having had the opportunity to know them well in their early married years.

III

I might be considered biased, since he was my wife's father, but I believe most people who knew him would agree that Spyros Skouras was a very unusual man. Born in the little village of Skourohorian in Greece, he came to the United States at the age of seventeen. He settled in St. Louis, where his older brother, Charles, had preceded him, and got a job as a busboy. Thereafter he and Charles and a younger brother, George, whom they had brought over to this country, organized a chain of motion picture theaters which they ultimately sold to Warner Brothers.

Thereafter Skouras worked successively for Warner Brothers, Paramount Pictures, and National Theatres, and in 1942 he became president and later chairman of the board of Twentieth Century Fox. During his later years with that company he took control of a small, financially troubled, American flag shipping company, which was owned by a friend, and after his retirement from Fox he moved his office to the shipping company, which by then had grown considerably in size.

Spyros Skouras's uniqueness did not lie in his business career, however. It is true that the companies he ran were successful and that he earned very large salaries for running them. But money for him was a means, never an end. It was something to be spent, to be given away, and to be plowed into imaginative new ventures, however distant the ultimate profit. The idea of husbanding his money, or investing it in safe and sound enterprises, was contrary to his whole nature. In a sense this was part of his greatness. If all the money at hand was spent, or given away, the cure was to go out and make some more to take its place. He was like the trapeze artist who lets go all the ropes and ladders as he flies through

207

the air, confident that he can catch another rope or another ladder on the other side of the arena.

But Skouras's true greatness lay in what he did for others. There was no cause to which he could say no. If it was a Jewish cause, he helped because so many of his colleagues in the motion picture world were Jewish and because he greatly admired Israel and his American friends of the Jewish faith. If it was a Catholic cause, that was his wife's church and one which he much respected. If it was a Greek Orthodox cause, that, of course, was closest to his heart of all. And if it was some down and out individual who needed a loan or a gift, Skouras was always ready to help, however low his own bank account might be at the moment.

One of Skouras's greatest hours was his part, with the help of the British and American governments and the Swedish Red Cross, in negotiations during World War II which resulted in the raising of the blockade of German-occupied Greece so that food and medicines could be admitted, and his leadership of the subsequent campaigns for funds to relieve the suffering people of that war-torn country. Yet he was an American first. He took his oath of citizenship seriously, and for all his love for his native land, it was to his adopted country that he gave his primary allegiance.

Above all else, Skouras was a man of the spirit. Always religious, he became more so as he grew older. The great Patriarch of Constantinople, Athenagoras, who in an earlier period was archbishop of the Greek Orthodox Church in New York, was one of his closest friends. It was his spiritual orientation as much as anything else which enabled Skouras to resist the ruinous temptations of Hollywood, which destroyed so many others who came in contact with them. Skouras's marriage to his beautiful and faithful wife, Saroula, was an unusually happy one; the fiftieth anniversary of that marriage was celebrated in 1971, a few weeks before he died.

It was through Spyros Skouras that I met Howard Hughes. Hughes is, of course, a legendary figure and was so at the time I met him. Born in Houston, Texas, in 1905, he was educated at schools in California and Massachusetts, ending up at the California Institute of Technology. In the course of a varied and turbulent life, he expanded the modest fortune he had inherited into what is now reported to be one of the greatest in the world. A daring aviator, in 1935 he established the world's land plane speed record and in 1937 and 1938 established records for transcontinental and around the world flights. In quite a different aspect of his career, he produced motion pictures with notable success. A handsome, romantic, dashing figure in his youth, by the time I met him he had already begun to turn into the lonely recluse that he is today. Even so, my contacts with him were altogether pleasant and, from my personal point of view, entirely satisfactory. He treated me with consideration, and I found him an interesting and sympathetic person.

Hughes trusted few people but one that he did trust was Skouras. There came a time in 1954 when Hughes was considering the sale of a portion of his vast properties, his purpose being to rid himself of the responsibility of ownership and management and to devote the proceeds of the sale to an ambitious project in support of medical research. Out of that circumstance there developed a series of preliminary discussions between Hughes and Skouras. Skouras in due course called in William Zeckendorf, the real estate developer. Responding to the indication of interest from Hughes, as relayed through Skouras, Zeckendorf put together a syndicate which at various stages of the ensuing negotiations comprised a number of different persons and entities, including Lehman Brothers, represented by Robert Lehman, Lazard Freres, represented by Andre Meyer, and Laurance Rockefeller.

William Zeckendorf is a colorful and flamboyant personality, who took over the staid old real estate firm of Webb and Knapp, expanded it to astronomical proportions and finally, by a combination of overexpansion, over-optimism and bad luck, saw it fall into bankruptcy. While it lasted, he ran his empire from a windowless, igloo-shaped, teakwood office designed by I.M. Pei, entertained his guests in a circular private diningroom perched above a Madison Avenue penthouse, and kept in touch with all his far-flung enterprises by telephones galore, including, of course, a telephone in his car. At his peak, he was a man of infinite energy, large imagination, and considerable charm. Even in adversity, he has retained much of those qualities, and is still operating from the igloo-shaped office, albeit on a more moderate scale.

The first time I saw Hughes was in Miami. Skouras, Zeckendorf, and I having gone down by plane, we were met at the airport by Hughes who drove us to a house on Biscayne Bay, between Miami and Miami Beach, which he told us he had rented solely for the purpose of providing a meeting place on this occasion. The discussion lasted for several hours and included rather specific references to properties and figures. Hughes was proving more difficult to negotiate with than the buyers had hoped, however, and not much progress was made at the Miami meeting toward the consummation of the purchase of his properties.

On another occasion a number of the members of the group Zeckendorf had put together, accompanied by two lawyers, set out to meet with Hughes in California. The lawyer representing Lehman Brothers and Lazard Freres was Arthur Dean, senior partner of the great Wall Street firm of Sullivan and Cromwell, who had been chief negotiator for the United States at the interminable peace discussions with North Korea at Panmunjom. The lawyer representing Skouras, Zeckendorf, and Rockefeller was myself. Rockefeller was also represented by John Lockwood, senior counsel for the Rockefeller family, but Lockwood operated largely behind the scenes and did not make the trip to California.

Our group went first to Beverly Hills, California, since Skouras had been informed that Hughes was staying at one of the large hotels in that area. After a time, however, Skouras received a message that Hughes would rather talk with us in some other locality. Accordingly, we were instructed to be at a certain corner at a certain time that evening, where we would be met and receive further instructions. I cannot now recall whether the whole group which had gone to California responded to these mysterious instructions or whether some of the members excused themselves. In any event, those of us who did respond, upon arriving at the appointed place at the appointed time, were ushered into a couple of small, inexpensive cars and driven to a relatively inactive airfield in the outskirts of Los Angeles. After being led into a medium-sized, twin-engine plane, we discovered Hughes sitting in the cockpit. After we had taken off for a destination still unknown, at least to me, with Hughes at the controls, he invited me to sit beside him in the co-pilot's seat. I asked him whether he was the only pilot aboard, to which he replied that the co-pilot was doubling as steward, which was what made the co-pilot's seat temporarily available. It was a beautiful starlit night as we soared into the California sky. The fact of sitting beside the mysterious Hughes and the fact that I did not know where we were heading made it an exciting occasion indeed.

As it turned out, we were headed for Las Vegas and the Flamingo Hotel. Although Hughes at this early date had not yet acquired the extensive properties in Nevada which he later bought, he did own the Flamingo Hotel, on one floor of which he had reserved for himself a suite of rooms. I myself did not participate in the discussions with Hughes at Las Vegas on that occasion, but I later learned that they were inconclusive.

My most interesting meeting with Hughes occurred in early October of that year when my clients sent me alone to Las Vegas to see him. Upon arrival in midafternoon, I was met at the airport by two members of Hughes's staff. Whether it is still so or not I do not know, but at that time Hughes was surrounded by a staff of clean-cut young men, all non-smokers and non-drinkers and mainly members of the Mormon Church. No sooner had I been taken to my room at the Flamingo Hotel by the staff members who met me than the telephone rang. It was Hughes calling to welcome me to Las Vegas, to apologize for not being able to see me at once, and to assure me that he would see me at the earliest possible time. I had heard stories of other people who had come to see Hughes whom he had kept waiting for days and weeks and of some, indeed, whom he never saw at all. I replied that I was quite relaxed and for him simply to let me know what best suited his convenience. He told me further that he had instructed his staff to take me out to dinner and to furnish any entertainment that I wanted. He wished to be sure, he said, that I was comfortable and entertained while I was waiting to see him.

Accordingly, two members of the Hughes staff and I dined in one of the other hotels on the strip, where we saw one of the extravagant floor shows for which Las Vegas is famous. Immediately after dinner, I asked to be taken home, since I had no idea at what hour Hughes might be willing to see me and I wanted to be available and as rested as possible when that time came. On the way back to the Flamingo, the staff members stopped to show me one of the most famous of the downtown gambling casinos, known as the Golden Nugget. It was designed like a casino of the old west, with dark wood and chandeliers simulating gaslight. It was quite a sight to see that room, with dozens of gambling tables surrounded by hundreds of men and women, grim-visaged and tense as they played the various games.

At about two o'clock in the morning I was awakened from a sound sleep by the telephone. It was Hughes calling from his rooms on another floor to ask me whether I had had a pleasant evening, and to apologize again for not being able to see me promptly. I had heard that Hughes often worked through a large part of the night, and here I had evidence of the accuracy of those reports. I again told him that I was quite relaxed, and for him simply to let me know what best suited his schedule.

The following morning was Sunday and, again for the reason that I wanted to be available at whatever moment Hughes should in the end select, I decided to go to eight o'clock mass. As I went through the hotel lobby at 7:30 in the morning, I observed that one of the roulette tables was still going, with a few dreary-looking persons still playing. I thought to myself how shocked my good wife would be if I were to tell her that I had played roulette on my way to mass. Accordingly, I stopped at the table and placed a quarter on number six. A quarter was the smallest amount one could bet at that table and I have always more or less considered six to be my lucky number. To my pleasure and surprise, six was the number that won, and I was paid off with thirty-five white chips, each being worth twenty-five cents. So excited was I by my winnings, that I forgot to take away my original quarter from number six until after the wheel had begun to spin for the next game. Having just won, I felt it would look cheap for me to remove the original quarter at so late a moment, and so I let it stay where it was. To my astonishment, number six came up again. What the mathematical chances of two such victories in succession are somebody else will have to figure out. In any case, by this time it was a quarter to eight, so I gathered up my new winnings, cashed in my chips, and went off to mass.

As I emerged from mass around nine o'clock, I noticed the Golden Nugget a few doors away down the street from the church. Having seen what it looked like at ten o'clock on Saturday night, I was curious to see what it would look like at nine o'clock on Sunday morning. The answer, as I discovered, was that it looked exactly the same. There were the same number of active tables, the same number of grim-visaged men and women, and the air was filled with smoke of comparable density. Looking on that sight made me grateful that, whatever other weaknesses and temptations I may have, gambling is not one of them.

Upon my return to the hotel, I was asked by members of Hughes's staff whether I would like to play golf. Since it was a beautiful day I accepted, and, with borrowed clubs and borrowed shoes, I had a very enjoyable eighteen holes on the grassy strip which constituted the golf course of the Desert Inn. Because Las Vegas is situated in the desert, the only parts of the course which were green were the irrigated fairways and putting greens. To the left and right was brown, unirrigated desert.

It was four o'clock in the afternoon of that day that I finally met with Hughes, a mere twenty-four hours after I had arrived in Las Vegas. I found Hughes an appealing if somewhat lonely figure. He was highly intelligent and almost courtly in his politeness. The fact of his deafness made him slightly difficult to talk with, but this was alleviated by the efficient use of a hearing aid. We talked for about an hour and a half. At the conclusion of the discussion, it was clear that he was still unprepared to react affirmatively to my clients' proposal. Seeing that I was disappointed by this result, he tried to compensate for it, on a personal basis at least, by asking whether he could help me with my reservations home. I accepted promptly, whereupon Hughes went to the telephone and made arrangements in a voice which I could not hear for me to fly first to Los Angeles and then, on an overnight flight, from Los Angeles to New York.

One of the staff members drove me to the Las Vegas airport, where I caught the plane by the skin of my teeth. There was one passenger, however, who arrived a few seconds even after I did and sank into the seat beside me, which was near the entrance. He told me that he was the owner of a successful small business in the Los Angeles area, who had driven to Las Vegas the previous Wednesday. As he drank and gambled, he began to lose heavily. When all the funds that he had brought with him were exhausted, he encountered some "friends" who advanced him additional money against the assignment first of his car and then of his business. When all that was gone too, his "friends" telephoned his wife in Los Angeles asking her to meet the plane on which, as their final act of generosity, they had bought him a ticket. Seldom in my life have I seen a man so dejected, with his car, his business, and his self-respect gone, and with his wife waiting for him at the gate at the Los Angeles airport.

Upon arrival in Los Angeles, I was met by the local manager of the air line, who took me to the ticket counter to check in. In those days transcontinental flights were slower than they are now and on overnight trips berths were provided in which a limited number of passengers could sleep, while the rest did their best to sleep in seats as they do today. As the manager and I arrived at the ticket counter, there was a man standing there whom I recognized as one of the leading Hollywood motion picture moguls. He was pounding the counter and demanding to know from the clerk behind it how it was that a berth which he had specifically confirmed by telephone at four o'clock that afternoon should now be unavailable. Remembering Hughes's quiet telephone call, I could, of course, surmise the answer. I am ashamed to say that my conscience was not bothered, however, as I slept peacefully in the berth which had so kindly been arranged for me.

In this general period there were many other contacts with Hughes by Skouras, Zeckendorf, and others of their group, in which one or more of the various principals participated. My personal meetings with him, however, were limited to the three occasions here described. In the end, of course, the negotiations came to nothing. Many years later, in 1972, Hughes sold an important portion of his properties in a public offering, the principal underwriter of which was Merrill Lynch, Pierce, Fenner & Smith.

CHAPTER EIGHT

Comparisons And Directions

I

At the end of a book of reminiscences, one should perhaps compare life in the earlier period with life in the later period. Where are we going, and are we better or worse off in the last third of the twentieth century than we were in the first third? It would take more than a chapter to examine those questions in all their aspects. What I propose to do is to draw some comparisons in three areas where I have had experience: education, the great law firms and banks of New York City, and, last, the city of New York itself. Finally, I will have a few words to say about trends affecting the presidency of our country and about the future of freedom in the United States.

World War II and the vast expansion of population and prosperity which followed it were the dividing line between education as I knew it in my youth and education as it is today. In New York when I was young, virtually everybody of any means lived in the city itself during the winter and sent his children to private schools there. The school which I attended from the age of nine to thirteen was St. Bernard's. It was run by two English co-headmasters and was wholly in the English tradition. Compared to the luxurious appointments of today's lavish suburban public schools, the physical facilities at St. Bernard's were spartan indeed.

For one thing, there were no showers, at least none that worked, so that the possibility of showering after exercise in the gym or in the yard simply did not exist. Lunch, usually consisting of a piece of boiled meat, a boiled potato, and some insipid boiled green vegetable, was put on the table at noon even though it was not to be eaten until half an hour to an hour later, so that by the time one got to it, it was stone cold. All school food is notoriously bad, but lunches at St. Bernard's during the time I was there were beyond the pale. Cruelty among the pupils, both physical and mental, was usual and accepted and old-fashioned discipline was the order of the day. Indeed, a student who was inattentive in class was as likely as not to have a soft indoor baseball or something similar thrown at him by an exasperated master.

Balancing the simplicity of the facilities, however, was an intellectual excitement and challenge which permanently shaped the minds of those subjected to it. Each year the school presented a full-length version of one of Shakespeare's plays, and this was done not in the school auditorium (indeed there was none!) but in a public theater. In the last three years of my attendance, the plays presented were *Merchant of Venice, Macbeth,* and *Hamlet.* Frederick

218

B. Adams, Jr., who later in life became the distinguished director of the Morgan Library, played Portia at the age of eleven, Macbeth at the age of twelve, and Hamlet at the age of thirteen. In the last role, he spoke thirteen hundred lines. It is hard to overestimate the effect upon one's attitude toward the English language of that sort of training.

Still another literary opportunity was a yearly contest involving memorization of one or another of Sir Walter Scott's great epic poems. One year it would be *Lay of the Last Minstrel* and another year *Lady of the Lake.* A pupil who memorized the first canto got an apple as a reward, for memorizing the second canto a pear, for the third a banana, for the fourth a box of chocolates and for memorizing all five cantos a bound volume of the works of Scott. How simple, but how gloriously effective.

The master who presided over these English exercises at St. Bernard's was Francis A. Tabor, one of the two co-headmasters. Mr. Tabor also taught mathematics. Since he loved English and only tolerated mathematics, and since I (for reasons hard to recall) was one of his favorites, I was often assigned during mathematics class to go to his library to select the reading for the English class to follow. As a consequence, while I have always had some reasonable facility with words, to this day I cannot balance my checkbook. Another recollection of Mr. Tabor revolves about the fact that he always had a glass of beer for lunch, even though the times were those of the Eighteenth Amendment when such consumption was prohibited, the beer being followed by a cup of tea. The interesting sidelight of this was his oft-repeated statement that the last time pure water passed his lips was at the age of ten, when he fell into a well and drank some inadvertently.

The next school I attended was St. Paul's in Concord, New Hampshire. St. Paul's, along with Groton and St. Marks and a handful of other boarding schools, were highly exclusive counterparts of Eton and Harrow and others of the English "public schools," which in fact were private. The term "public school" as it was and is used in England is in differentiation from being tutored at home.

At St. Paul's the great emphasis was on character, on friendship, and on conforming to certain traditions and practices which separated those who were "accepted" from those who were not. The difference started in a sense at birth, because it was at birth that one was "entered" at the school; that is, one was put on the list for going there when one had arrived at the age to qualify for one of the lowest two "forms," which was what classes were called. The two lowest forms were the equivalent of seventh and eighth grades. Boys who had not been entered at birth could still go to St. Paul's, but for them to get in they had to achieve a substantially higher grade on their entrance examinations than boys who had been so entered.

An absolute requirement for social acceptance at St. Paul's was a cold shower before breakfast. Anybody who was known to avoid that ritual, however subzero the temperature outside, was a pariah. Since for most of the boys the dining hall was a considerable distance from the dormitory, it was not unusual in the winter to see boys who had not had time to dry their hair arriving at breakfast with their hair frozen into solid icicles. No wonder that the infirmary prospered in those cold months.

Another absolute requirement for social acceptance was to change one's clothes in the afternoon, to get out of the jacket and tie one wore to class and to put on "old clothes." In most cases this meant participation in some organized sport or at least a brisk walk to Jerry Hill or to Long Pond. But it was not the exercise as such that society demanded. While one was not admired if one spent the afternoon in the library, one could do so and get by, *provided* one did so

220

in old clothes. In a school then numbering some four hundred and fifty boys, there were perhaps six or eight at any one time who flouted this requirement, and they were total social outcasts.

Along with all this demand for conformity came an ease of human relationships and a formation of friendships which in many cases have endured for the whole lives of those concerned. Moreover, since everybody shared the same facilities and lived the same schedule at school, differences in financial backgrounds between students were a matter of which one was totally unaware. There were a fair number of students who were on scholarship and who paid less than the full cost of tuition and support, but nobody knew who they were. There were other students who came from enormously rich families, richer by far even than the fairly comfortable median, but nobody paid any attention to that either. A few years later in our lives—to some extent at college and certainly thereafter—those financial distinctions mattered, but at St. Paul's they mattered not at all.

Compared to all this, or alongside all this, we have today the great public school system. Forty years ago public schools were places of relatively limited quality where one expected to get the rudiments of reading, writing, and mathematics, with some basic science and maybe a little language in high school, but not much more. Today, especially in the suburbs surrounding New York, they are emporia of magnificence unequalled in all educational history. Financed by vast bond issues, the taxes to support which weigh heavily upon those who have to pay them, they have physical facilities which make the richest private schools of today—let alone of yesterday—seem poor by comparison: auditoriums, laboratories, athletic fields, and other accoutrements which stop short only when talented architects, expansive-minded school boards and compliant taxpayers come to the end of their imaginations or their resources. Teachers at today's

public schools must meet all sorts of demanding requirements, and in most cases they have master's or doctor's degrees. Their pay almost without exception exceeds the pay
of teachers at even the richest of private schools.

In trying to assess which system is better—the unfettered,
relatively spartan, "noblesse oblige" type of private school
which dominated education one or two generations ago, or
the physically luxurious, bureacratically structured public
school to which the overwhelming majority of Americans today go—one has of course to consider the changed circumstances of our national life. With the growth of population
and the expansion of prosperity, the oldtime private school
could not possibly take care of today's need. Indeed, the oldtime private school has itself changed. Today the private
schools, like the public schools, are generally coeducational.
The process of differentiation between students who were
"entered" at birth and those who were not has totally disappeared. And intellectual competition and independence of
thought have to a large degree displaced the overriding demand for social conformity. The fact is that both aspects of
our educational system have responded to the needs of the
times, and this is good. On the other hand, what we have
today in essence is a tendency to egalitarianism, to a common denominator between public and private education.
Whether this egalitarianism is a step up or a step down in
terms of its ultimate effect upon our society is a question
upon which opinions will differ. Perhaps only time and
history can provide the answer.

II

A somewhat similar trend has taken place in the great New
York law firms and the large New York banks. As was true

with private schools, the leading law firms of forty years ago and the leading banks were citadels of inherited privilege and the exercisers of very great influence on our society. Today there are many changes in those situations.

When upon graduation from Princeton I decided to go to law school, the obvious course would have been to go to Harvard. Entrance into Harvard Law School for anybody who had a decent undergraduate record at Princeton, Yale, or Harvard was in those days no great obstacle, and Harvard Law School was the obvious and accepted open sesame to a job in one of New York's top law firms. Maybe one could get the New York job from Yale Law School or Columbia, but Harvard was the most clearly defined route.

I decided, nevertheless, to go to Virginia for my law degree. I decided this in part because of my attraction to one of the professors at that school, Garrard Glenn, who was the father of a friend and contemporary since my days at St. Bernard's, and who had had a distinguished career at the New York Bar before joining the Virginia faculty. In other part, I went to Virginia because my instinct was to be different, and I had enough confidence in my ability and my family's social position to feel that I did not need the Harvard degree to open the doors for me in New York. I never regretted going there; indeed my three years in the lengthening shadow of "Mr. Jefferson," as he is invariably called there, were among the happiest of my life.

Nevertheless, it was a decision which at the time took some courage, or foolhardiness if one prefers that term. The situation in that respect was somewhat improved a few years later when Franklin D. Roosevelt, Jr., the son of the incumbent president of the United States, chose to go to Virginia Law School, and further impetus was given to Virginia's standing when President Roosevelt selected his son's graduation as the occasion to make his famous "the hand that held

223

the dagger has struck it into the back of its neighbor" speech, referring to the declaration of war against France by Italy under the leadership of Benito Mussolini.

Today the situation is dramatically different. Today the top New York City law firms draw not from Harvard Law School only, or even from Harvard, Yale, Columbia, and Virginia, but from dozens of law schools across the country. Not only do they draw from those other law schools, but those top law firms have organized systems for proselytizing which can only be compared to old-fashioned rushing for college fraternities. Each fall they send their partners fanning out across the country to interview at law schools from coast to coast, in some cases sponsoring expensive social gatherings for members of the graduating class and in almost all cases paying the expenses of students whom they invite to New York for further discussions. Indeed, so harsh has the competition for the ablest young lawyers become that the principal law firms and the placement offices of the principal law schools have drawn up rules governing recruitment procedures, somewhat like the Geneva Conventions governing "civilized" warfare. Some law schools have even established their own special, additional rules and regulations governing recruitment on their campuses which, if violated, result in the violating firm's being blacklisted from recruiting there. One well-known firm having been either unable or unwilling to live up to the rules at Harvard set up a recruitment office across the street from the campus, from which location it carried on business as usual until a couple of years later when it was restored to grace.

Beyond all this, of course, and as a result of it, there have been vast changes in the great New York law firms themselves. Where forty years ago they were to a significant degree made up of descendants and relatives of earlier partners or of members of the families of important clients, today they seek talent and ability wherever they can find it. Forty years ago, saving only a few firms which were notable and recognized exceptions, the partners of the blue-chip Wall Street firms were overwhelmingly white, Anglo-Saxon, Protestant and male. Today there is no top firm without several partners who do not fall into those categories.

With the great New York banks, the story is similar in some respects but different in others. In the early days of the century, the New York banks dominated the financial life of the country. Largely unregulated by government, combining as they did both the deposit and lending functions on the one hand and the securities underwriting function on the other, it is no wonder that the senior J. P. Morgan could meet with the president of the United States almost as an equal. It is also no wonder, given their vast power, that the banks in those days attracted to themselves many of the brightest and most ambitious young men who were graduating from college, especially if they came from the right college and the right family background.

But today there have been vast changes. In the first place, banks are now among the most regulated of all industries. They are subject not only to the banking departments of their respective states or to the Comptroller of the Currency, depending on whether they are state chartered or national banks, but also to the Federal Reserve Board, to the Department of Justice, and to a myriad of other governmental agencies. The Securities Act of 1933 has firmly separated the deposit function from the underwriting of corporate securities. Beyond that, the great New York City banks, which once were the only financial bridge between American business and world trade, now have to compete with regional banks in Chicago, San Francisco, Dallas, and other cities, which have vastly expanded their influence in recent years. The nation's largest bank, for example, is no longer in New York but in California. Finally, the banks have to compete with a number of other non-banking institutions which have achieved prominence in the lending field, including insurance companies, finance companies, and others, as well as industrial corporations which lend out their surplus funds in the form of "commercial paper."

A consequence of the regulation of banking and the proliferation of the lending function is that banking has become less attractive to the able, ambitious young man. However, under recently enacted laws banks are being permitted, through bank holding companies, to expand into non-banking but bank-related activities, and this will hopefully restore some of the vitality which the New York banks, through no fault of their own, have lost in recent years.

If anything I have said in this chapter gives the impression that in New York City the "Establishment" has given way to total egalitarianism, let me hasten to correct the impression. Egalitarianism has gained much ground, and in the years to come will almost certainly gain more, but as of now there is still an establishment and it is still to be reckoned with. The Council on Foreign Relations, for example, still comprises the main leadership in foreign affairs of the private sector, its distinguished membership drawn from government, industry, the academy, the great foundations, and the top law firms. The Century Association, a private club occupying a beautiful Stanford White building on West 43rd Street, gathers at its monthly meetings and at its daily "long table" what is probably the greatest aggregation of intellectual influence in the country—in the arts, in the foundations, in the universities, in the professions. The Association of the Bar of the City of New York, the most elite of the bar associations, exercises a long-term and behind-the-scenes influence in legal, judicial, and legislative matters well beyond the force of its mere numbers. Then there is a whole clutch of social clubs. There is, for example, The Links, a luxurious and pleasant private club in the East Sixties where self-made businessmen foregather to break bread and share a drink with each other and with representatives of "old money" dating back to the club's founding in the early years of the century. The list of establishment organizations could obviously be added to: the Cosmopolitan Club, which is a sort of female counterpart of The Century; The Brook, which is like The Links but with a little more emphasis on the social side; the Harmonie Club, most of the members of which are prominent in the Jewish community; and many others. Yes, we are in an egalitarian era and yes, that tendency is growing. But human nature does not change, and persons with the inclination for social exclusiveness or the capacity to influence their society will continue to band together in various organizations for those purposes.

III

One of the principal institutions of my lifetime which has remained essentially unchanged is New York City itself. It may have changed in detail. Clearly there have been physical changes: new buildings, new highways, new bridges. Maybe it is a more dangerous place to live than it used to be; certainly it is a lot more expensive a place; but in its essence it has survived the years. Recently I have had the opportunity to reflect upon this subject because one of my duties in the law firm where I sit is to help in the hiring of new young lawyers, most of whom are about to graduate from law school, and to discuss with them the pros and cons of working and living in New York.

Obviously there are lots of arguments against living in New York. First of all, there is the cost. Rents are appalling, the price of transportation, whether subways or buses or taxis, goes up with painful regularity, and the temptations of the city's cultural assets are themselves not without their price. Most significant of all the arguments against living in

New York, perhaps, is the cost of bringing up a family there. With very few exceptions, the public schools of the city are not places where anybody who can afford an alternative would send his children, and not only are the costs of private schools prohibitive but the facilities of available private schools are so limited that in some cases only one out of ten applicants can be admitted. Indeed, to get a child into Brearley or Chapin or Spence (girls) or into St. Bernard's or Buckley or Collegiate or Trinity or St. David's (boys) or any one or another of the relatively few existing private schools in New York sometimes seems harder than getting into the *Social Register* or into *Who's Who*.

Most people who are in a position to do so have solved the problem by moving to the suburbs. But how much they have missed by making that decision! New York, more than any other secular institution I know, has retained its glory through the years.

Many of the city's advantages are obvious—its museums, its theaters, its ballets, its restaurants, its opera—these are the benefits of living in New York which are always cited. They are great benefits and I do not derogate them, although from experience I sometimes wonder how many people who live in New York actually take advantage of them and how often.

The fact is, however, at least in my opinion, that living in New York has many advantages beyond those so often cited. For one thing there is its history. By that I do not mean only the buildings which have been designated as landmarks by the Landmarks Preservation Commission, although there are many such buildings and they are indeed beautiful. Nor do I refer only to the fact that New York was for a brief period the capital of our young country or that General Washington said farewell to his troops in Fraunces Tavern, which still stands on Broad Street in lower Manhattan.

The history of New York which truly distinguishes it, in my view, is the history of its people, together with the current, living manifestations of that history. New York is the early Dutch who came here with Henry Hudson, and the early British who later took their place alongside the Dutch, and the Sephardic Jews who settled here before the American Revolution, and the German Jews who joined them after the 1848 uprisings in Europe, and the Polish and Russian Jews who came over in the early years of this century. New York is the Irish who fled from the potato famines to build its streets, its tenements and, above all, its churches, and it is the Italians who came later to challenge the Irish supremacy. (It was not until after World War II that there was an Italian leader of Tammany Hall, the citadel of political power, or an Italian mayor, or an Italian bishop of the Roman Catholic Church in the New York Archdiocese.) New York is also the Puerto Ricans and the blacks, native-born citizens of the United States, some of whom have acquired positions of leadership, but all too many of whom still perform the menial but essential tasks of our throbbing economy. New York is the Greeks and the Chinese and the Cubans and the myriad others who have come here from other lands, and it is also the strong men and women who have moved here from other sections of our own country to assume positions of leadership in the corporate and financial enterprises headquartered in Manhattan.

But it is important to recognize that New York is much more than Manhattan. It is also one- and two-family houses in the Bronx and in Queens, in Brooklyn and in the borough of Richmond. It is the small homes on Sheepshead Bay and at Throg's Neck, under the shadow of the Triboro Bridge, where people who commute by subway or bus to their jobs as bank tellers or construction workers or waiters or salespersons own their little but well-kept boats moored nearby in the swirling, beautiful and, alas, for the moment, contaminated waters of the East River, which for all its name is not a river at all but a channel connecting the Atlantic Ocean with Long Island Sound.

Yes, of course New York is filled with dangers: there are muggings and drug addicts and the streets and parks are risky and the rich live behind doormen and the poor behind triple locks with large dogs. But what of the suburbs? The drugs are there too and, while the muggings may be fewer, there is often a kind of boredom and emptiness and intellectual sterility there which grips the spirit at least as ferociously as the city mugger grips the throat.

The fact is that New York City, just as it has been for all my lifetime—even more than it has been for most of my lifetime—is today the crucible where the future of our society will be determined. This is not to say that the smaller cities and towns of our country are not important; obviously they contribute influences of significant magnitude. Nor is it to say that the farms are not important, although their number is dwindling annually and the farms which continue to exist are tending to acquire corporate propensities. But it is to say that the large cities of our nation, and above all New York, which is the archetype of cities, represents more of the good and the bad, more of the rich and the poor, more of the intelligent and the stupid, more of the divine and the diabolical than any other segment of our society. If that society is to survive it must survive in New York. Put the other way, unless our society survives in New York, it will not survive, at least in my opinion.

Lest some should consider my views in this respect too controversial, let me move to a less controversial aspect, a consideration of New York's physical beauty. There are many gloriously beautiful cities in the world: certainly Paris with its boulevards and its monuments, Rio de Janeiro with its white habitations nestled in the crevices of the mountains which surround its harbor and with its giant Christus looking down from the towering Corcovada, and San Francisco with its combination of water and bridges and hills. But if anybody has any doubt about the physical supremacy of New York, let him come in by plane at dusk as the millions of lights in the city are being turned on, or let him go on a clear day up the West Side Drive and view the magnificence of the Palisades as they tower over the estuary of the Hudson River.

If those experiences are not enough, let him take the ferry from Staten Island to Manhattan, still in this day of inflation costing only five cents. On that twenty-minute ride, he will see one of the greatest commercial harbors of all time; he will pass the heroic Statue of Liberty raising her torch to "the huddled masses yearning to be free"; he will see the baroque ruins of Ellis Island, the way station through which millions of immigrants who helped build our country passed in penury and in hope. Finally, he will see the massive skyline of the greatest material monuments ever created by the hand of man, beside which the pyramids of Egypt and the Colossus of Rhodes pale into insignificance. And, if he is lucky, as my wife and I were on a recent such ferry ride, he will find two volunteer musicians, a violinist and an oboist, playing a Bach cantata on the main deck of the ferryboat and making music which in the simplicity and magnificence of the circumstances seemed to rival the angelic chorus.

IV

Of all the areas of change and contrast in the forty years of my adult life, one of the most important has been in the political and governmental arena. The developments which I here have in mind are the growth of the power of the presidency, the decline of the power of Congress, the decline of the power of political parties, and, finally, the increasing threat of inflation. These developments raise interesting questions, in my opinion, concerning the future of the democratic system and of political freedom as we have known it.

Through all our history there have been strong presidents and presidents who were more passive. To some extent this has followed a swinging of the national pendulum: from a weak Buchanan to a strong Lincoln and back to the weaker presidencies of the years following the Civil War. The first really strong president of modern times was Theodore Roosevelt. Many examples could be cited of how he wielded his strength, one of the best known being how he dealt with Congress on the issue of sending the fleet around the world. It will be recalled that when Congress was reluctant to authorize the funds for that voyage, Roosevelt sent the fleet halfway, for which he had the funds, and left the problem to Congress as to how to bring it home. The pendulum swung back with the passive presidency of William Howard Taft, swung forward again with the war leadership of Woodrow Wilson, and then back again under Coolidge and Hoover.

Beginning with President Franklin Roosevelt, however, the pendulum has remained well on the strong side of center. There may be some who would raise questions in this respect concerning Truman and Eisenhower, but I do not think such questions are justified. Truman's actions in the foreign area—the decision to use the atom bomb, the Marshall Plan, the Truman Doctrine, the dismissal of General MacArthur—all these were strong and decisive actions. Likewise, in the domestic arena, his leadership in civil rights, the firm manner with which he dealt with a threatened national railroad strike in 1946, and above all, his successful 1948 campaign for reelection, in which he ran against the record of what he called "the do-nothing eightieth Congress," were all the actions of a strong president.

Eisenhower's method was different. Having been trained in the military tradition, he tended to operate through chiefs of staff—John Foster Dulles in the foreign field and Sherman Adams in the domestic area. But the president took pains to retain control over the ultimate decisions, and in any case Dulles and Adams were extensions of his authority rather than representatives of any competing power center. The record of the Eisenhower years, incidentally, looks pretty good in retrospect: prosperity and reasonable tranquility at home, and abroad, the successful interventions without war in Guatemala and Lebanon, the bloodless confrontation with Communist China in Quemoy and Matsu, and, above all, a wise refusal to commit the nation militarily in Vietnam. Eisenhower's natural reservations concerning other forces which tended to infringe upon the presidency— as, for example, in his farewell warning against the long-term threat of an uncontrolled military-industrial complex— were those of a basically strong leader.

President Kennedy's term of office was too short to evaluate in this respect, but clearly Lyndon Johnson was in the category of strong presidents. With President Nixon the issue has reached the front pages of the news. As a result of his management of the Vietnam War, of his impounding of funds previously appropriated by the Congress, of his periodic retreats from press conferences and other contacts with the public into semi-isolation, of the vast growth of the White House staff and the consequent lessening of the influence of the cabinet, the whole question of the power of the presidency as compared to the power of other segments of our government and of our society has come to a kind of climax.

Short term, it is possible that Congress may put some restraints on the president's powers, especially in the light of the Watergate crisis and its aftermath. Long term, however, it is my opinion that the tendency of the presidential power to grow is one that will not change but will continue. There is a confluence of many factors pushing it in that direction. Among these are the vast resources available to any president in his staff and in the government departments which he controls, the enormous leverage of the patronage that flows from his appointing powers, and the fact that in the area of foreign policy his position is clearly constitutionally dominant.

Congress, by comparison, is largely limited to negative and delaying actions, and even those powers are frequently more theoretical than real. It is required to advise and consent with respect to treaties, but increasingly presidents have acted by executive agreements rather than formal treaties. The Vietnam cease-fire agreement of January 1973 is only one example. Even more importantly, Congress is limited by its resources of staff. Where the White House has virtually unlimited resources of personnel, the individual senators and representatives as well as the various committees are limited to staffs which are negligible by comparison.

It is true that in some areas the Congress has leverage. The refusal by the Senate to confirm two of President Nixon's appointments to the Supreme Court and his later appointment of a director of the FBI, are cases in point; and with respect to other presidential appointments, such as federal district judges, the "personally obnoxious" doctrine still gives a senator a veto over some nominations in his own state. But in larger matters the contest between Congress and the White House is strikingly unequal. For the Congress to stand against a president it must form an alliance among the various members of the legislative body which is difficult to create and even more difficult to preserve, especially as the president uses his veto powers and all his patronage powers to divide and conquer.

One of the factors of modern life which has contributed largely to the growth of the power of the presidency is television. Not only does a president have the power to act in any situation, but he is in a position to benefit from the publicity which that action generates. Not only do his acts dominate the newspapers and the television news shows, but he has the right and the power to get free coverage in prime time for pronouncements which he, in virtually his sole discretion, deems to be in the national interest. There are times when the opposition party can ask for and get free time in reply, but even when this is granted the impact of the news is usually past and the spokesman for the opposition, being a representative of a group rather than a principal, is apt to be relatively ineffective.

A counterweight to the growth of executive power has been the Supreme Court. Since the day when the court overturned important measures of President Franklin Roosevelt's New Deal, it has been a force with which occupants of the White House have had to reckon. In the long run a president has considerable influence on the Court through his power of appointment, but there is a natural lag resulting from the fact that generally the majority of the Court at any given moment is made up of appointees of administrations previous to the one then in office. There is also the significant historical fact that, once appointed, members of the Court do not necessarily vote in accordance with the views of the man who appointed them. Thus in the 1972 decision with respect to the constitutionality of state laws forbidding abortion, three of President Nixon's four appointees took positions opposite to the public position which the president had taken on the same issue. But the issues on which the Supreme Court is called upon to function are narrow and few by comparison with the broad range of issues upon which a president acts. For all its ultimate power in the relatively narrow range of its responsibilities, the Court has at most a marginal restraining influence upon the growing power of the presidency.

Historically, one of the restraining influences upon the presidency has been the political parties. Indeed there have been times—the relationship between Mark Hanna, who was then the dominant Republican political leader, and President McKinley is an example—when presidents were clearly responsive to the political leadership which created them. But in the eighth decade of the twentieth century political parties do not carry the weight they once did, and this too is adding to the powers of the presidency.

In appraising the influence and method of political parties in the United States, it is important to understand their makeup. The fact is that there is no such thing as *a* Republican party or *a* Democratic party. What we have in the United States are fifty Republican parties and fifty Democratic parties, one in each state. Thus, the Republican party in states such as New York, New Jersey, and Connecticut is one thing, while the Republican party in states such as Arizona and Indiana is quite another. The same is true of the Democratic party. There is very little relationship between the Democratic party of Massachusetts, Alaska, and California and the Democratic party of Virginia or Louisiana.

So far as the presidency is concerned, what happens is that every four years the various state-based parties send their representatives to a national convention to select a candidate by bargain and compromise. Once the convention and the subsequent election are over, the machinery is disbanded, except to the extent that a sitting president may exercise some cohesive influence by the force of his personal leadership and the power of his patronage. The national committee of each party performs various mechanical functions, but has almost no influence on policy or on the selection of future candidates.

The fact that politics in the United States tends to be basically centrist is a result, in part at least, of the machinery through which those politics function. Each of the major

236

parties has its conservative wing and its liberal wing. In order to find a candidate who can command a majority of a national convention, it is therefore necessary to find one who can satisfy at least the less extreme members of both wings of the party. The healthy consequence is that in the selection of candidates the extremists on the right and the left tend to be left out, with the candidate usually representing a compromise and therefore a basically centrist view. Inasmuch as the same general process goes on within both major parties, the end result is usually the selection of candidates who, because each of them is basically centrist, do not differ significantly from each other. A further consequence, also healthy, is that because there usually is very little significant difference in the policies of opposing candidates for the presidency, a change in government requires relatively little adjustment on the part of the country. In the exceptional instances where the centrist tendencies have been overridden, as in the nomination of Goldwater by the Republicans in 1964 and in the nomination of McGovern by the Democrats in 1972, the party making such nomination suffered disaster in the succeeding election, thus virtually ensuring a return to centrism at the next convention.

There are some who believe that our political system would be better off if all liberals were in one major party and all conservatives in the other, so that the voters could choose between ideologies. In my view any such a "realignment of parties" would be most unfortunate. It would risk the possibility of the kind of ideological fractionalization of parties which has so frustrated the governmental process in some European countries, and it would lose for us the tendency toward centrism which has served us so well.

Because our political parties are based at the state and local level, it is there that their strengths and weaknesses must be examined, and it is there that we find their influence sharply declining. This has arisen in part because government welfare programs have replaced much of the personal service which political organizations used to give to their clients and which provided the leverage to hold the loyalty of those clients. A second factor which has contributed to the decline of the influence of political parties is television. Before the days of television, most voters rarely saw a candidate for top office face to face. Accordingly, they tended to get much of their information about him by the kind of word of mouth upon which a well-organized local political apparatus could have considerable influence. With the advent of television, however, candidates for major office can in effect sit in each voter's living room and appeal for his vote over the heads of and without regard to the views of the party machinery. Finally, the growth of the direct primary has contributed to the same result. In New York State, for example, it used to be that candidates for governor and senator were chosen exclusively by conventions and conventions, of course, are relatively easy for politicians to control. Under a recent law, however, a candidate receiving twenty-five percent or more of the votes of his party's convention is automatically empowered to run in a primary election and thus has the opportunity of overturning the convention's decision by a direct appeal to the voters.

The net effect of all these influences is to greatly enlarge the power and influence of the man who occupies the White House and, to a lesser but significant degree, the power of the executive heads in the various states, the governors. Whether on balance this is good or bad will have to be judged by history. Given the complexities of our modern world, it seems to me that it is more good than bad, with one important proviso. That proviso is that we continue to have freedom of press, radio, and television. With the decline of the influence of Congress and of the political parties, the opportunity of the voter to get the true facts through the communications media becomes more crucial than ever. Should this ever be materially curtailed, either through the improper exercise by the government of its television licensing powers or through an acceleration of the kind of economic pressures which have caused the demise of so many newspapers in recent years, or otherwise, the dangers to our freedom resulting from enlarged executive power could become very real indeed.

Finally, consideration must be given to the matter of inflation. Inflation in the modern world arises from many causes, but basically it comes from the fact that societies are spending more than they produce. When an individual follows this process, there is a day of reckoning; he simply goes broke. With governments, however, the consequences of inflation can be at least partly concealed and the day of reckoning can be postponed by the monetary printing press. There are flurries of trouble on the way, such as adverse balances of payments, currency devaluations, and other difficulties, but a strong and productive economy somehow keeps going in spite of them. However, by the constant recurrence of such troubles, they tend in the long run to grow in magnitude and seriousness. The time may well come when truly painful adjustments will be necessary. Whether a popularly elected Congress, responsible to voters who can throw its members out of office, will have the fortitude to impose the painful remedies which will then be required is a question only time can answer. It is more likely that in such a crisis the country will turn to a strong executive. Since he, too, under our present system can be voted out of office, there arises the further possibility that the crisis—or the succession of crises—will call increasingly for an erosion of some of what have heretofore been considered our basic economic freedoms and maybe even some of our constitutional rights. Indeed, there are some who believe that that process is already to some degree underway.

As one looks about the world and as one reflects back

through history, one realizes that freedom as we know it in the United States is a very rare fact. Its existence today is limited to a few western and western-oriented nations constituting a clear minority of the peoples of the world, and even there it has existed for only some two hundred years out of all the thousands of years of recorded time. Any assumption that this rare and fragile condition will continue indefinitely even in the United States would be a rash assumption. Indeed, civilization itself is a thin veneer, through the polished crust of which the lava of chaos bubbles from time to time, as in the ghetto riots of a few years ago in the United States, as in the horrors of Northern Ireland's civil war, as in the inhumanities perpetrated at My Lai, as in the "tiger cages" and other prisons of Vietnam, both North and South, and as in more other places and instances than one would wish to remember.

On the other hand, there is no *necessary* reason for freedom to fail in the United States or for the crust of civilization to be permanently broken. The descendants of the people who created these priceless conditions can preserve them if they wish to do so. For this to happen there must be first of all a recognition of the reality of the threats which confront us. Next there must be a national willingness to perform the acts of self-restraint—economic, political, philosophical, and personal—which will control and subjugate those threats. Finally, we must adhere with unbreakable persistence to the sense of optimism and confidence in our destiny that, together with our resourcefulness and our industriousness, has made us what we are today. If we do all these things, our system and our way of life will continue to flourish in the future as it has in the past. The persons described in this book have been the architects of large segments of our successful past. I have no doubt that others like them will be the successful architects of our future.

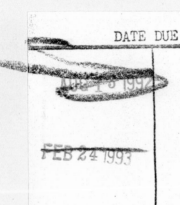